LOVE IS A DANGEROUS WORD

For Margaret and John.
Best wishes from
Maggie.

Love is a dangerous WORD

Maggie Dukes

Zaccmedia

Published by Zaccmedia
www.zaccmedia.com
info@zaccmedia.com

Published May 2017

ISBN: 978-1-911211-52-5

British Library Cataloguing-in-Publication Data
A catalogue record for this book is available from the British Library

Some names have been changed to protect their identity.

To my late husband, Bryan Dukes. A happy man...

CONTENTS

ACKNOWLEDGEMENTS

To Mary Millard, my good friend who did the first edit, and to my family.

FOREWORD

by Paul Steeples

Summer 1977. I was 15 years old. Unable to live with my mother, and with my father living abroad, I needed somewhere to stay for seven weeks until my father returned to the UK. A friend at school suggested I might be able to stay with him at his home, Old Rectory House, Radipole. ORH, as it was sometimes known, seemed as nice a place to spend a few weeks as anywhere else I (or my social worker) was likely to find. A large house, with a huge garden and a river running through it – this would be a lovely spot to spend the summer. I would stay for the few weeks, keep out of trouble (as much as possible), and say my goodbyes and move on to the next phase of my life. Little did I know that those few weeks would change my life forever. This was a house full of love, joy, laughter and tears, a family home and so much more. All were welcome and so many seemed to come. There was something about Old Rectory House that was different from anything I had ever experienced. After those few weeks I knew that I had probably, for the first time in my life, found a home. Having no Christian background, the 'religious' aspect of the house seemed a little strange, but I could not help but be overwhelmed by the way everybody was treated with so much love and respect, literally all ages from cradle to grave.

Yes, I left after my initial seven weeks, but Old Rectory had become my home and Margaret, Bryan and their children had become my family. I returned every school (and later college) holiday to spend time at ORH. Something about it seemed to nourish the soul. It was only later after committing my life to Jesus that I realised that ORH was a place where God's love was very much in action.

Old Rectory House was not some Disney palace where the sun always shone and never a cross word was spoken. It was real, it was gritty, and it dealt with real-life problems and with tragedies. It dealt with those issues by applying the love of Jesus Christ in the most practical of ways. Old Rectory House was a place where faith, love and deeds co-existed side by side.

I have so much to thank Margaret and Bryan for. You will find out more of my story in the pages of this book. I hope as you read this 'story' you will get some sense of the adventure that Margaret and Bryan went through in their years at ORH. The whole thing defied logic, it should never have worked, and it should have been a financial and social disaster. But it was an adventure with God, and his love shone out from that home as a beacon to a sometimes dark world.

INTRODUCTION

This is the story of Old Rectory House, Radipole, Dorset, between 1974 and 1990. Many of the people in the story are still part of the church in Radipole. I have remembered things which happened, situations and events which were incredibly real and true. I may have made some mistakes, so if you remember anything differently as you read this, please contact me, and we'll put them right together and I will apologise to you if necessary.

The dictionary defines nostalgia as 'a bittersweet longing for those things, persons or situations of the past: the condition of being homesick'. In a way the same could be said of this story. Certainly there are people in the story who are missing now, those whose place can never be filled, in this life at least. The dear old house, the beautiful garden and particularly the people who lived there are always remembered by those who knew them with a feeling of nostalgia and homesickness. However, time moves on and we must move with it, or forever be left behind like a lot of fossils when in fact we should be acting as vibrant, useful human beings, whatever our present circumstances. So let us not be morbid about the memories stirred up in this tale. Let us keep our eyes on Jesus, the author and finisher of our faith! We must be joyful people, living in today, and only look on past happenings in a positive way.

I have heard it said that history is written by the winners. Well, I consider myself a winner as I embark on this extraordinary account. It ended in some personal tragedy, but the same could be said of many who sincerely answer God's call to do His kingdom's work. Just think and consider what happened to Jesus! We talk glibly about following in His footsteps when we are young, but they lead to a cross. (Didn't Jesus say 'Take up your cross'?) But the cross was not the end – after the cross comes the crown. There was the *resurrection!* So, in Him, we're always the winners.

Before I begin the story, I must emphasise that it is about what God has done; it is not for anyone to boast about. As Jesus told us, we are just His unworthy servants. The principle and vision of Old Rectory House was always that it must show God's love to the world around it in a practical way. To *be there* was enough. I cannot understand why things happened as they did, but I have written them down as my memory takes me back to events. As I have been writing about them, the situations have made me contemplate the biblical teaching behind them, and at the end I comment on what I have learned.

Although I have written in the first person, it is not just about one person or one family. It is about a small group of people who grew into a crowd. We all had our part to play in God's purposes. It is an account of what happens when a fellowship of God's praying people put their faith into action. I do not want to give an impression that any one person or group of people can take the credit for anything done in this story. It is part of His story. It must all be to the glory of Jesus' wonderful Name and not ours. We wanted to affirm the worship of our churches, and aimed to bring people into the life which Jesus gives through them. We always tried to support our church in every way we could, and brought everyone who stayed with us to the family service each

Sunday while they were our guests. We also tried to give priority to requests for people to come and stay which came from our own clergy and congregation, but this was not always possible if the house was already full.

The names of some people in this account have been changed in order to protect them. I have tried, wherever possible, to contact those whose stories appear, so I hope that there is nobody who is hurt or offended by seeing their story in print.

I must also impress upon my readers that this is an account of past things, and every mistake we made or anything hurtful that happened has been dealt with before God. All negative things have been forgiven. Our church is still a vibrant, thriving community of sincere worshippers. We learned such a lot from the hard times, but now we live in the present; in the tension between the 'already' and the 'not yet'. We remember the words of St Peter:

> … though now for a little while you may have had to suffer grief in all kinds of trials. These have come so that your faith … may be proved genuine and may result in praise, glory and honour when Jesus Christ is revealed.
>
> (1 Peter 1:6–7)

Some of the young people who became believers while staying at Old Rectory House are still active members in their home churches, including the Radipole parish. Some are musicians and worship leaders; others preach or lead services; some are in teaching ministries and youth work, and in their turn are leading other young people to come to faith in Jesus Christ. Who can tell what things God has done and is still doing with the little bit of faith put into action by some very ordinary people who went beyond reason and followed Him into this rather crazy project?

On a more personal note: what was it that motivated a couple in their forties, who had known some very hard times in bringing up their four children into their teenage years, and who at long last had reasonably well-paid professional jobs, to embark on a sea of uncertainties and throw it all away just when prosperity was beginning to become a reality in a small way? There can be only one answer to that question. It's the same response as any missionary or minister of the gospel would give. It is a compelling vision of what God was asking them to do. They *had* to follow, or forever know they were hypocrites, only giving lip service to their Lord. It took a major battle to come to terms with the reality of the call, but it has never been regretted, wherever the adventure finally led them.

I have heard it said that the fact of knowing that we are where God wants us is a great motivator. That was our testimony from the very beginning. So here goes… Into the story of Old Rectory House.

CHAPTER 1

HOW IT ALL BEGAN

In 1970 a Church Army mission came to Radipole. It was the first of many, but it was very fresh to us then. We were a rather staid church, still suffering from the after-effects of World War Two. It was suggested that every lunchtime during the week of the mission, people could come to the church and pray for a few minutes. My husband Bryan and I went. With others, we knelt in the pews, and silently prayed in a manner which we had never experienced before; we were all very shy of each other. On the Thursday, something happened to me which was to change my life forever, although I didn't know it at the time. It was all done in secret. A quiet 'voice' began to ask me questions and make statements, of which I had no idea before.

'Do you love Me? I must come before anything or anyone else in your life. I must be more important than your job.' (I had a new job as a district nurse and I loved everything about it; especially the lovely colleagues, some of whom are still my friends now.)

'You must put Me before your house, your car, your new wage, your status and everything which matters to you.'

'You must put Me before your friends and family – your children.' This was getting near the bone – I adored our four children and would defend them before anything else.

'You must put Me before your husband Bryan' – now I was in big trouble! I didn't want to admit, even to myself, that Bryan was the most important person in my whole life, and I loved him even more than God Himself. I struggled and squirmed and fought a battle there on my knees in church.

'Yes, Lord, all right, I will put You first,' I finally responded, exhausted.

We went home for our quick cuppa and a little lunch. We had just ten minutes, and I told Bryan what had happened in church. As we were talking the phone rang. I often had a call to ask me to see a new patient in the afternoon. However, this call was different.

'This is the community car organiser. You have been allocated a new car. I'll be around in ten minutes…'

I already owned a Ford Anglia car, which although it was a bit old, was the first one I had ever had all to myself, and it seemed wonderful. The new car arrived, and it still had the plastic over the seats. It was so new – just 80 miles on the clock. I was over the moon, but apart from the thrill of the new car, I knew it was an answer to the challenge put before me in the church only a few minutes previously.

How amazing! What was happening? As time went by, I would discover more of the Lord's plan for my life and the changes which would happen, especially concerning the Old Rectory House.

CHAPTER 2

OLD RECTORY HOUSE – A HOUSE OF DREAMS

Old Rectory House, the house where we went to live and work, had been the rectory of the parish of Radipole, Weymouth, Dorset, for at least a hundred years – since Victorian times until the time we arrived and took up residence. It must have stood there for many years before that as a yeoman farmer's house, as was evident when one looked at the old doors and the layout of the place.

It was a large rectangular house, with Edwardian sash windows and French doors at the front, and the entrance on the east side, which looked down the long drive to the road. It had been cleverly built so that it had sun most of the day in the summer and a blank wall to protect it from the westerly gales in the winter. It faced straight down the River Wey. This was so that in past times, ships coming up the estuary could see a light in the window to guide them to the harbour if it was dark.

In Roman times there was a harbour in Radipole village, but this has not been used since the river silted up many, many years ago. Proof of this harbour lay in our friend Molly's house, Letterbox Cottage, next door but one, where the remains of a Roman road could be found in her garden. This once ran straight to Dorchester, 8 miles north.

The house was constructed from local stone and had a slate roof. Two dormer windows sat on the roof of the second floor. They were skilfully renewed during the time we lived there by our friend Peter Kirby (as was the bannister and the staircase). A very large Velux window was cut into the back of the attic by a kind roofer friend who came to mend the roof. This transformed the two attic rooms, making them so much more accessible. In time they were used by many of the young people to whom we gave a home.

When an architect friend came from Christchurch with a view to making plans for extending the house in 1987, he was intrigued to discover that the foundation stones on which the house stood were very large. Almost certainly they were taken from the Roman harbour, which was once at the riverside.

The whole of the front of the house was covered by Virginia creeper which turned red in the autumn. Over this grew a large wisteria plant, which had been on the wall for a long time and bore a profusion of bright blue flowers in June and July. Flower beds surrounded the base of the house. So it was altogether a very beautiful, old-fashioned house, just the place to relax in! One gentleman visitor (Revd Stanley Scriven) commented when he came to stay with us for a much-needed break, 'It's just like being in heaven!' It was a well-deserved comment.

The grounds spread over nearly 3 acres, with the River Wey running the length of the south side of the paddock. There was a large lawn in front of the house, and the flower beds were surrounded by a mixture of mature trees and bushes. As well as the paddock, there was a sizable vegetable plot. The earth was pure alluvial soil and made for prolific growth, so that home-grown vegetables were produced for cooking, most of the time we lived there.

As the years progressed, flowers grew in profusion, starting the year with carpets of snowdrops, followed by all the spring flowers growing under a very large chestnut tree, which stood on the left of the drive. It was acknowledged to be the largest in the area. In the autumn, hordes of children would arrive with big bags to collect the conkers!

But although the place was so beautiful, we were there for the people, not to farm the land. We would have liked to have kept some livestock there, and in fact we did keep chickens – most of which were eaten by the fox! We also had several hives of bees; although I had kept these for years before we came, having so many children in the place potentially could have caused problems if they had become too interested, so the care of the hives was handed to local beekeepers.

I would dearly have loved to have kept a couple of donkeys there. I dreamed about how we could attract the children with donkey rides and fun. Also, Irene, a dear lady farmer who often stayed with us, used to tell us how we could keep a couple of calves during the summer, sending them to the abattoir in autumn and this way having enough beef to fill the freezer for the rest of the year. However, this never happened.

CHAPTER 3

A THRILLING MOMENT

Old Rectory House – the house of dreams! Before the dream could be realised and the house become our home, I needed to work out my notice as a district nurse, a position which I had held for many happy years.

During this waiting time it became my habit to drive into the garden and take a little time to pray. One morning, I sat on the steps at the front of the house, the lawn spread at my feet like a green carpet. The overgrown garden seemed to be waiting to be brought again to life and productivity. Behind me, the old house sat in silent decay.

I have mentioned that the house was really old with a long and amazing history. That story would fill a book on its own! It seemed that the house was almost pleading for someone to come and rescue it. The whole place was full of ghosts. How many people had sat in the very spot where I was sitting at that moment? In my imagination I could almost see genteel Edwardian ladies playing croquet on the lawn, or pompous gaitered gentlemen thinking up their next sermons, sitting on a garden seat under the chestnut tree.

Almost a hundred years previously my husband's grandparents had worked there in the house and garden. He himself, as a 15-year-old, was organist and choirmaster at the little church of St Ann's, which was just up the road. In the 1940s Bryan was required to stand to attention in the rector's study (later it was used as a bedroom for folk who required nursing care) while he was told which hymns had been chosen to be sung at the Sunday services. In due course he, for many years, had the joy of choosing them himself and planning the Sunday services.

Soon we would see real, lively people running around the lawn, chasing the dog and having fun and games. However, that day, as the silence deepened, little creatures gained confidence and came out to continue their lives as if I was not there at all. Birds of many kinds, rarely seen these days almost five decades later, flew in and started to strut on the lawn. At least two green woodpeckers came; there was also one with a red head. Several rabbits appeared, and a squirrel or two. I expected a deer to walk through the bushes and start grazing on the long grass. I haven't seen any of these creatures there since the first years that we lived in the house.

In my imagination the place was asleep, just like Sleeping Beauty's castle in the fairy story. I had just dropped in on my way to work that morning, stopping by to pray, because I had a dream. It would not let me go. It was a very expensive dream. It would take everything and, maybe, everyone I valued. But I knew it was from God Himself, and I could not afford to ignore it. His words drummed incessantly in my head.

'Obey Me, and you'll see My glory shine – in your own home town and among your own people.'

I sat there for the few moments I could spare, hoping that the Lord would give me some comfort and confidence for the task ahead. I tried to listen, but it is not easy to clear the mind when one is on one's way to work, with the day's busy schedule clamouring for attention. Nothing but silence… Then…

'Do you remember the little boy who gave his picnic to Jesus?'

Had I heard correctly? I could hardly believe it. I had asked God to speak to me, but when He did, I had very little faith to believe that He really had. How often does He speak to us and we don't respond because we don't have enough faith to accept that He really did address us? We then miss the thing which we are longing to hear. It wasn't until after my response that He spoke to me again. After a while I answered, 'Yes, Lord.'

'That boy only had five loaves and two little fishes, and just look what Jesus was able to do with them! He fed five thousand people! If Jesus could do so much then, He can do just as much with your little offering. Don't worry about anything. All will be well. Trust Me!'

I bowed my head. 'I will, Lord,' I answered. 'I believe You. Help my unbelief and my weakness.'

I went on my way rejoicing that day. My heart burns with the thought, even now.

I continued to dream. On 6 June 1974, my husband and I took our daughter to Oxford in our Austin 'maxi' car. She had an interview at the John Radcliffe Hospital, where she later trained to be a nurse. As my husband drove the car I sat watching the countryside go by. I began to dream. I saw our rectory, which was then a quiet, very private home, hidden by trees, in a very different mood.

I saw it full of people. Many of them were friends from our church. I did not recognise any individual friends except our rector. He came out of the French doors behind the steps where

I was sitting. He was singing and laughing. This was strange and rather lovely, as I suddenly realised that I had seen him do neither of these things for a very long time.

Then, I saw that some of the people in the picture I was looking at were sad, lost people with grey faces and carrying big burdens. I began to get some meaning from the dream. These sad people needed to experience God's love in practice. Words were not enough. Christian people needed to love them, as Jesus loves them, in His Name. They needed caring for in a practical way, Christians being 'Jesus' to them and meeting their individual needs as He directs through the Holy Spirit's power.

We needed to be a praying people, who must be ready to listen to each person, listening at the same time for His direction regarding each situation as it arose. We were to give these people a break from the pressures they were under. We were to identify with them, rejoice with them, and without pressure to lead them to the Lord – the healer of all hurts.

This vivid dream would not go away. Over the next few days it grew and became clearer. Eventually I shared it with Bryan. We prayed about it and awaited the Lord's leading.

On the following Sunday at church, someone lent me Watchman Nee's book on Nehemiah. I took it home and began to read. Immediately it began to speak to me. Looking in my Bible, the words I read seemed the very words of God to me, confirming my dream.

'Rebuild the walls; pray for the sins of Israel, my people. Identify with them, get down on your knees and confess' (taken from Nehemiah 1).

I began to understand. Where sin goes unchecked, we are responsible.

The whole story which I am about to relate in this book can be written in the context of the book of Nehemiah. Other scripture confirmation given to us at that time was Isaiah 58:6–12 and 2 Corinthians chapter 4.

Another book which came into my hands in a similar way to Watchman Nee's was *The Hiding Place* by Corrie Ten Boon. I had heard Corrie speaking on a radio interview one Sunday morning and had been very inspired by her answers. Her books still inspire me to this day, and at that time God spoke to me every time I picked one up to read it.

CHAPTER 4

THE DREAM IS SHARED

As Bryan and I talked about the dream and the new spiritual depth into which we felt God was leading us, we decided that it was time to share it with our rector.

One unforgettable afternoon I walked with him in the sunny little field behind our house as we took our dog, Zeta, for a walk. I told him everything. He responded with wonder and joy. I think, looking back, that he really needed a new vision himself, as he was going through a time of great discouragement. None of us knew at that time that he was seriously ill, and within the next year would undergo major surgery.

He suggested that he should start looking for another house in which to live, since he was due to retire in the near future, and the rectory would then be sold by the Church Commissioners. He said that he could do a better job if he lived nearer the church. Then he suggested that we start to share the dream with more people and set up a fund to raise the money to buy the rectory.

In amazement I heard myself say, 'We need three years before we go there.' Whatever made me say that? I wanted to start right away! Later on I felt sure that it was the Holy Spirit who prompted me to make that statement, as subsequent events proved that this was God's timing. We must follow His agenda, not our own. His timing is always the right timing. During this period, as we waited, we carefully shared our thoughts with trusted, praying friends, and eventually, as it became known what we had in mind, we were able to tell more and more people. Most of these gave very positive encouragement. It was obvious that a caring home was very badly needed in our area. It became a major subject for prayer in our church and among friends we had in other churches in our town.

On 12 July 1974 there was a 'Songs of Praise' evening service at the small, ancient church of St Ann's, which is the mother church of our parish. My husband was to play the organ for this service, so I went, taking our four children with me. One of their friends read the scripture lesson. We sat in the front pew, just under the pulpit. All the way through the service I was acutely aware of the Lord's Presence. The air seemed as clear as are the hills when the sun shines after the rain. I found myself worshipping Him in a way that I had never experienced before. For me it was entering a new dimension. As we knelt for the final blessing before the recessional hymn, I knew I was kneeling at the feet of Jesus! His Presence was so magnificent and awe-inspiring that I did not dare to move or even breathe. I could not look up. Very shaken, I stayed rooted to the spot as the choirboys began their procession out of the church. As I forced myself to my feet, the rector was following them and he looked at me with complete understanding and empathy. Perhaps he had had a similar experience at some time – we all have our spiritual 'tale to tell'.

We came out of church into a perfectly beautiful summer evening. The family wanted to go to Abbotsbury beach where mackerel are caught in nets and pulled up on to the pebbles. Everyone who is there is invited to help, and after the fish are all safely landed the fishermen sell them. We always bought some, intended for the next day, but usually they were eaten that evening for supper as they are so delicious when freshly caught.

We all piled into the car. The dog had waited in it while we attended the service, so it was a very full car! There was no problem as we didn't have to worry about seat belts in those days. I sat in the back with our youngest son on my lap (he was 12 years old at the time!). Our teenage son sat in the front with the dog, and the two girls squeezed together beside me. No-one complained about the crush. It was all good fun. We were a really happy family.

I felt as if I were in a little world of my own that evening. It's a memory clearly etched on my mind, for it changed the whole course of my life, which has been richer and more vibrant ever since.

As we drove across the hills towards the beach – a distance of about 8 miles – we came to the spot where the road turns a corner and there is a lovely view of the valley. At that moment I had a wonderful vision of people everywhere in the air. The whole sky was full of them. They were in heaven – or somewhere happy and peaceful. There was the most beautiful scent or fragrance in the air, and such wonderful music that it is impossible to describe it. I could feel, rather than see, my dead mother's presence, and some of the people I had loved and 'lost'. I just cried and cried for joy. No-one in the car noticed! My dear family were always so concerned if I was just a little bit sad about something, even though I rarely needed to cry in those days. Life was so very sweet.

In a sort of trance that still no-one seemed to notice, I opted to stay in the car when we arrived at the beach. The family all went down to the water with their fishing tackle and the dog. I sat watching them and trying to pray. I was really concerned about them. Was I being a responsible wife and mother, following all these strange ideas? As I sat thinking about all this, I saw a rainbow of glowing emerald light cover the entire family as they were silhouetted against the sea, in the shadows of the encroaching evening. They all stood side by side in a row, with the dog at the end. (Just recently, even since writing this, while reading Revelation in my Bible I was amazed, even shocked, to see that St John saw a similar picture in his vision! Could I have read this before my 'beach picture', and my memory brought it into my mind? I do not know or understand. All I know is that what I have told you here is genuine.)

These people were so precious to me. There was so much to risk if we pursued this dream.

I heard, 'Don't worry. They are safe with Me. The fishes in the sea are all Mine.' In my dreamy state I thought I saw fishes swimming around in the sea!

'The cattle on all the hills are Mine.' I looked behind me and saw the cows grazing on the hill.

'I will supply the money, the workers, and everything you need. Just trust Me!'

These words, being given so soon after what had been a special service, on this very special evening, have given me confidence and strength on countless occasions since. When life was hard at the house, money short, when tempers were hot and the pressures pushing very hard; then the Lord reminded me of my own special and very private 'commissioning'.

CHAPTER 5

DOUBTS, FEARS AND FINANCES

Over the next few months, indeed over the next couple of years, privately we had to fight a great battle. I discovered first-hand what is meant by the 'attacks of Satan'. Often I would wake up at three or four o'clock in the morning and spend an hour or more walking through our little house in confusion. I would stand at our landing window, looking out at the garden and the great elm tree which stood behind it in the fields that we all loved so much. A big black cloud of depression and uncertainty would enfold me until I could hardly breathe.

What was I doing? Was I becoming mentally ill; imagining myself into a situation that was all of my own making? Or had I really heard the voice of our Almighty Father God? Did He really want me to pursue this dream?

One day I went into the church to pray. I was at an all-time low.

'I'm just a fool, Lord,' I moaned. 'I'm bringing my lovely family to ruin through this dream. I'm in such a state of confusion and distress. Please help me – I'm just a fool!'

Out of the silence came a quiet voice.

'God's fool,' it said.

'All right, Lord, if I'm a fool for You, that's all right with me,' I answered. 'If You want to stop this, please do so. I'll just go on and trust You to lead or to stop me as You wish.'

I had a very happy and satisfying lifestyle. Our marriage was really good. Bryan and I were still very much in love after twenty-one years of married life together. It hadn't been easy with four little children to bring up on a small income. But what amazing children! They were the delight of our life. At this time in our lives, they were all in their teens and we were still a devoted, close-knit family group, with no major problems such as some parents – people we knew – were coping with.

As well as my home life, I also had a career. I had trained as a nurse before my marriage, and since the children were grown and coping well with their lives I had taken a post as a community sister. This was a thoroughly enjoyable experience for me. I had a brand-new 'Health Authority' car to drive around in; a phone at home for the first time; a certain amount of prestige and status, and a lovely new smart blue uniform! I also had very pleasant and agreeable work colleagues. When we were not 'out on the job', we came up with plenty of ideas for fun and outings. Above all this, I enjoyed the money! It meant that our family were better off than we had ever been. We had begun to extend and furnish our house in a very pleasing way.

We had not forgotten the endless struggles we had previously known at the end of each month – but now we had two nice, fat pay-packets coming in and it was wonderful.

How could I give this up after so many years of near poverty? And how could I ask my dear husband to give it up, too? Was I mad?

I enjoyed my bit of status, my new responsibilities and my contact with the public so much. Some of my patients could be difficult, but many were a joy to visit. Job satisfaction was a new experience for me, and I found it especially powerful when dealing with the patients who had terminal illness. I approached the care of these people with all the love that I could. To me, this was a Christian ministry as much as any other 'full-time work'. How can I ever forget the deep impressions these patients made on my life as they approached the end of their mortal lives? Working with them became a real proof to me of the hidden resources God gives to those who trust Him, while those with no definite faith usually viewed death with abject terror. Even if bravely concealed, the tension in the air in those homes made me shudder inwardly. In contrast, I went to some lovely, peaceful homes where the presence of Jesus was so beautiful, even in the midst of terrible suffering. I felt uplifted and helped by the privilege of ministering to these people.

Now I was being asked to give that all up and become a housewife again, with no income, no status, and as I have since proved, be the butt of all the jokes and the one who had to do all the nasty jobs that no-one else wanted to do!

My response was, 'No, Lord – please don't ask this of me. I can't do it. It's too much to ask. What about all the further training I've just been offered, with the possibility of a glamorous job as a practice nurse in my doctor friend's new surgery? What about the lovely little house we looked at, which has just come on the market? We could all be so happy there…'

But the dream persisted. In my spirit I heard, 'Obey Me! Others can do those jobs. I have so many houses. You'll see My glory shine.'

As time went by, things began to look black. Our beloved rector had cancer of the throat. It seemed that there was no chance he would fulfil my wonderful dream now. Indeed, I felt sure that he would never sing again. He became more and more sick. One terrible night, in the very house that I had dreamed about, he had a massive pain in his chest and collapsed at three in the morning. His wife phoned for a doctor, but it was the weekend. Their own doctor wasn't on duty. My doctor friend was called out instead. It was his third 'call-out' that night and he was exhausted because he had just returned from visiting someone else. Later, his wife was to tell me that she helped him into his clothes, gave him the address and instructions, and pointed the car in the right direction, hoping he would wake up on the way! The house was out of his usual 'patch'. He also told me later that he thinks the car drove itself. He doesn't remember how he arrived at the house, but although he was so tired, he made a correct diagnosis in a very difficult situation. The rector had a ruptured aortic aneurysm. This was almost always a fatal event in those days – a sentence of imminent death. The ambulance was called, and all the correct hospital procedure was set in motion to be ready for immediate surgery, if there were to be any chance of saving his life. It was 1976 and such heart surgery was still in its infancy. The nearest hospital which could accommodate him was 40 miles away in Bournemouth. On the way to the hospital the ambulance needed to stop because the paramedic could no longer hear a heartbeat or feel a pulse. (There were no fine machines to monitor those things then.) After efforts to resuscitate him seemed to be useless, and just as they were about to abandon the attempt, he began to revive! The surgeons were waiting for him in the theatre and they operated immediately. They gave him a new, strong aorta with a plastic tube round it, which was to keep him safe for the next ten years!

Ten days later the rector came home from hospital. His wife phoned me and asked me to visit him. Rather awed at the prospect, I presented myself at the door.

The rector met me with open arms and a reassuring smile!

'I know your dream is true now,' he said. 'I will do everything I can to make it happen.'

CHAPTER 6

THINGS PROGRESS

If he were still here, the rector would tell you himself of the wonderful happenings on the night he was taken ill. Only one month after this great adventure, he insisted on getting up in his own pulpit to tell his congregation about what he had experienced.

He said he had met with the Lord when he was unconscious in the ambulance and going to the hospital. He really wanted to go with Him to be where He was, but the Lord told him there was work for him to do before that could happen. Part of that work was to make it possible for this special dream to be fulfilled!

As time went by and the rector recovered, we saw a great change in his attitude as well as his health. He became a really cheerful man with a sense of humour that we hadn't experienced before then.

'Call me "Eric the Cleric",' he told the people in his congregation.

We began to hear him sing and make fun. A fete was arranged at the rectory the following summer. He had a sideshow all to himself. It was 'Guess the length of my scar!' This was the one resulting from the huge surgery he had undergone for his heart operation. It went over his shoulder and down his back (a very different matter to the keyhole surgery performed in this day and age). The picture I had in my dream of a rector who laughed and sang was emerging! This was also a confirmation of the dream's authenticity.

Financial arrangements were made to buy the Old Rectory from the Church Commissioners. Their asking price was £30,000. That seemed a lot of money in 1976, but only twenty-five years later it was sold for something like £300,000. Now, in 2017, it must be worth a million or more!

It is worth noting here that although we moved in and the work rapidly moved forward, the Church Commissioners did not confirm the sale until one year later, on 1 November 1977. We wondered if we would be required to pay rent for our occupation during this time or if we would be accused of 'squatting' in Old Rectory House. Also, all through this first year we still did not know if we would be able to afford the payment, as the bank rate had risen by an astronomical amount to 15% in 1977, and we needed to borrow a third of the total amount from the bank. We really were thrown into an exercise of faith. The other two thirds were coming from the sale of the curate's house which was no longer required, and the sale of our semi-detached house plus some generous interest-free loans made by people who shared our vision – but the final third was still outstanding.

On the very day the sale went through in London, although we were not informed until a while later, there was an offer from 'St Gabriel's trust fund' in Weymouth to donate £10,000, which did not have to be paid back except for 4% interest per annum, paid quarterly. The trust was now an administration only, as the St Gabriel's Home had been a maternity project to help unmarried mothers but had closed down a long time previously. (I found this quite significant, as I had fostered two babies from there until they went for adoption. Our own children were the reason we did not foster any more babies than these two, because our whole family suffered so much when the time came for them to leave for their new homes, as we had grown to love them very much and wanted to keep them.)

This offer from St Gabriel Trust was a great boost to our faith, as we saw God's hand in what was a wonderful financial miracle. It was the timing which was so especially wonderful. God's timing is perfect, as we often discover. We worry unnecessarily, when all the time He is quietly planning something better than we could ever have imagined.

However, to go back a little in the story… Before we made a definite decision to move to Old Rectory House we took our four teenage children out to dinner and put the whole idea before them. We had always shared any major decisions with them, and now we explained all that the move might entail. Our income would halve, so they would have to make sacrifices. Their privacy might be lost, although we promised them a room to themselves while they lived at home. They would still be in *their* home and we would not forget their needs; they would always be a priority to us (and they still are). Our room would be a private one with a television, where they could shut themselves away if they wished. We promised to take them out to dinner once again in two years' time and discuss as a private family how they really felt about living at ORH (as we abbreviated 'Old Rectory House'), and if they were really unhappy about it we would move out.

It always gives me a thrill to remember that two years later, when we reminded them that the time had come to go out for a dinner and discussion again, they all happily agreed to an evening out, but didn't want to go without our special foster boys, Neil, Paul, Jerry and Ian.

'There's nothing to discuss, Mum and Dad,' they all said. 'You know it's the best thing we ever did as a family and we never want to think about leaving!'

By this time in their lives, they had all made their own professions of faith and were eager new Christians.

Before we began to pack up and leave our home we all went for a lovely family holiday in a boat on the River Thames. It was a wonderful way to celebrate our unity as a family and stood us in good stead for the many adventures we were to encounter in the years that lay ahead.

On 20 September 1976 the rector and his wife came to our house with a key to the rectory. Retirement had come sooner than they had anticipated. They had moved into their new home just the day before – enabling us to move further into the adventure with God which awaited us.

CHAPTER 7

STEPPING OUT IN FAITH

I shall never forget that first evening after we had been handed the key. Bryan and I went down on our own to explore the old house. It had been a balmy September day and the air seemed to contain a breathless quality – a sense of unreality, as if we were in a dream.

The dream which I had had two and a half years previously was turning into a reality before our eyes.

Those early days at the Old Rectory House were so beautiful and awe-inspiring. They were really the very climax of our happy life together. It was as if, up until then, in all of our lives we had been working and walking towards that time. The memory of them is precious indeed.

Until we actually had the key to the door we had not allowed ourselves to think too much about the house. It was, after all, someone else's private home. We needed to concentrate upon the work and ministry to be done, and not dwell too deeply on material details and excitements.

The old house, which was to become our home and the scene of so many 'ups and downs', seemed just like a fairy-tale castle, Sleeping Beauty's castle!

As we drove up, the car brushed the bushes either side, all the way up the drive. Their branches towered above us as they joined together. Everything was so overgrown it was almost like pushing our way through a tunnel. The large lawn was neatly kept, but around it on every side other briars and bushes were greatly overgrown, and also the elm trees which bordered the entire length of the River Wey. These became victim to the Dutch elm disease which had spread throughout the country, devastating the lovely trees, so they were later felled by the River Board and their timber given to us for fuel for fires, which lasted all the years we lived there. The elms were replaced in time by willow trees, which didn't grow too high during our time there, so we were able to enjoy the fine view. The road behind the house was also lined on both sides with elm trees, which were diseased like the ones by the river. These were also felled by the local council and replaced by others. When all the elms had gone, the light poured in, making the place seem much bigger.

Bryan and I went inside the house. It was in a terrible state and looked such a daunting prospect! Where the rector's lovely antique furniture and beautiful paintings had been, faded patches now revealed the state of the walls. Each way we looked it was so shabby and tired. Mice were also a major problem. One could smell them everywhere. In the two attics at the top of the house we found an odd assortment of ancient articles which had long been forgotten and were well past their use-by date! There were two wheeled 'Bath chairs', suitable only for a museum, and a clutter of small objects which, if they could have spoken, would have told us many a tale of long ago. There was a croquet set, very old and faded, with wooden balls. The sight of these things is what probably fired my imagination when I sat in the garden later.

Outside, the garden was even more amazing. Hidden in the undergrowth we found rusty iron railings, behind which the paddock grew waist high with comfrey and many other weeds in wild profusion. Still further back, threatening to engulf everything, were more briars and thorn bushes. We could not even see the river, which we knew ran at the boundary of the estate, and on either side of which stood the old elm trees covered in ivy. Although this account sounds exaggerated, there were many beautiful things in the garden, too. Several mature trees were growing, which, when we started to clear the undergrowth, showed that they had been planted and planned, in days gone by, with a view to a future lovely garden. As mentioned before, a wonderful great chestnut tree dominated one side of the garden. It was a listed tree, and the best free-standing chestnut tree in the borough. Many other beautiful trees surrounded the lawn and graced the grounds, including a mature fig tree and a copper beech.

It was 6 December 1976 when we hired a van and moved our bits of furniture from the little semi-detached house where we had been so happy, and took them to Old Rectory House. Twenty-three people turned up from church to help! Our belongings all looked so inadequate once we had unpacked them. We put the boys' things in the two attic rooms, which had been cleaned and repainted in preparation for this great day. Our daughters would share a room when they came home from the hospital where now they were both training to be nurses.

The following day was Sunday. As Bryan was the organist and choirmaster at the church, we decided to leave early in the morning. We walked down the drive, where quite a lot of clearance work had already been done. In fact, a 'digger' had spent a couple of days uprooting a number of large saplings, and a car park area had already been made. It was a still, icy morning. White frost covered everything, and we were breathless with excitement!

The very next day things began to happen so quickly that we felt we were on a roller coaster of activity. The Bath chairs that had been in the attic never actually reached any museum! I looked out of the landing window to see one of them being pushed frantically down the drive by a crowd of laughing choirboys, with more boys sitting in it on each other's laps. Before I was able to do anything to rescue it, the old frail chair fell apart into too many pieces to ever be put together again. The boys laughed and laughed! Several things like this 'bit the dust' before I could do anything about preventing it. The whole place exploded with people and the hum of busy activity and life. I had to remember that those people mattered more than the things.

However, what fun we all had! How we sang and how we laughed together – and miracles began to happen.

CHAPTER 8

THE BODY OF CHRIST IN ACTION

Everyone who worked at Old Rectory House, including ourselves, was a volunteer. Right from the time we decided that the old rectory should be used for Christian care, this wonderful volunteering started. So many people came to give a hand that no-one became overly stressed by too much work. Indeed, a great many people came to help and we were all carried along by the tremendous conviction that God was at work in the project, and we all wanted to be a part of it.

When we first went to live at the house, the garden was just a jungle. As I described earlier, to reach the house one had to drive through a tunnel of trees and bushes, as the path was almost completely overgrown. Although he had tended the lawn, our dear rector had been too ill to do anything else. One of the first things, therefore, was to clear this and make a car park. A few days after we started the preparations before actually moving in, a big digger arrived. I'm not sure now where it came from! The whole place sprang into action. Men seemingly appeared from everywhere, and we could hear sawing and see the growing piles of logs for firewood, providing fuel for the fierce winter which was to come. (We didn't know that it would be so cold, but God did!) The car park 'happened' as if by magic, and we needed it more and more as people started to visit us. Then in 1977 there came the sad demise of the elm trees, and the replanting of the willows, all done by the River Board and making things so much safer and better for us.

Next, along came our dear volunteer painters with their brushes and buckets. Gardeners, too, appeared from nowhere. Some we knew, but others we had never met before. I remember one such man who arrived with a chainsaw and told us that he was a tree surgeon, and would we like him to deal with some unwanted branches and wood? Would we? Yes, please!

Before that first weekend was over we had lots more light in the place, plus a lovely pile of firewood to feed the hungry open fires all winter. With the work done, the tree surgeon disappeared. Was he an angel? Or was he a man who wanted to help a project which spoke of God's love and made him think? Whoever he was, we like to believe this was so.

Another man and his son, painters and decorators by trade, came with huge tins of magnolia paint and spent their weekend transforming the tired, dark landings and stairways into a bright, cheerful centre to the house. They were very shy about their work, and sadly, didn't invite conversation with anyone else in the house, but they came and did a wonderful act. Who can tell what God did in their lives through this act of kindness? It's not for us to know. A lot of really hard, manual work was put in by so many men that we couldn't start to tell their names because the list would be too long.

Of course, ORH was a very old house, with all the accompanying difficulties. Mice ran everywhere when we first moved in, and our cat, Purkiss, had a wonderful time catching them. However, he had a habit of bringing them to us half dead, and dropping them at our feet!

Some of the rooms were very cold and draughty and the central heating was almost non-existent. After a while, the damp invaded the very small kitchen, which grew 'mushrooms' on the wall in some places. The kitchen floor consisted of big flagstones, hard to keep clean and easy to trip over. We did, however, manage to live with this for ten years, after which the new kitchen was built.

The downstairs bedroom was made from what had been the rector's study. We used this to nurse people who were unable to manage the stairs. It was both small and inconvenient, with no plumbing, so no facilities for nursing patients, but we managed all this with a lot of cheerful laughter and goodwill from everyone. The knowledge that God had sent us there and was carrying us along reminded us that St Paul had said he could be content whatever the circumstances. We were all so happy, because as a poster said, which greeted everyone as they arrived at ORH,

> WE ARE AN EASTER PEOPLE AND HALLELUJAH IS OUR SONG!

The poster was on the wall over the door, opposite the entrance to the house. Little bigger than A3 in size, it depicted the three crosses on the hill where Jesus was crucified, with the rising sun behind them and the empty tomb in front.

No spoken words were needed. Words can be detrimental when your heart is bursting with pain, as many hearts were when people first arrived.

On the landing upstairs, on a green background with a picture of lilies of the valley, another poster stated,

> LOVE GROWS HERE

Other posters and pictures, some of them painted and given by people of the church, made appropriate hints in a harmonious and pleasant way, so making a time at the house a time of being soaked in positive and helpful messages, cheerfully given. Some of the people visiting the house were devoted Christians; others didn't state where they 'stood' as regards spiritual matters, but they mingled happily with a common purpose and vision – to make a place where people who needed that extra bit of care in an informal setting could receive it with 'no strings attached'; no pressures to join something they did not as yet understand.

CHAPTER 9

GOD'S AMAZING PROVISION

One of the first things which happened very soon after we had moved in was a small army of ladies arriving with sewing machines and curtains from their own houses.

'We needed new curtains in our sitting room/bedroom/landing,' they said, laughing as they told us. Soon the measuring tapes were out, and scissors could be heard cutting cloth. Gradually, old curtains were transformed into lovely new curtains, which really, in fact, were not new at all. When they were put up they graced the old windows in a way that could not have looked better even if there had been brand-new ones.

When the menfolk arrived with pots of paint and wallpaper, I asked them, 'Where did all that come from?'

'Oh, I told the salesperson at the shop that we needed it and why, and he just gave it to us!' was the answer.

Even with new paint and curtains, we still needed furniture. Very soon the phone started ringing and people were telling us that they had furniture or carpets to spare because they were getting new things. Could we use them? Could we indeed! When things arrived we were constantly amazed because they were just right for the old house. Room after room became painted, curtained and furnished, making a lovely, happy home just right for hurting people to be soothed.

While we were making the house habitable for the new work it was to do, a strange thing became evident. Whenever it was decided that a certain room should be the next one to be redecorated and carpets and furniture were needed in order to make it habitable, the phone would ring and someone who couldn't possibly know what we needed just then would be offering exactly the right things to fit that room. The first time this happened we all exclaimed about the coincidence, but as it happened time and time again, some folk became silent as they contemplated this strange phenomenon, and the Christian folk began praising the Lord! When paint was given to us by local firms, it always seemed to be the colour which we had suggested for that room, and carpets sent to us were the right colour, too. We sometimes had to cut them up and stick them together to fit the room, but they looked great.

One time a cooker and then a fridge arrived, and also a very useful plate-heating cupboard, which fitted exactly into a space in the kitchen which would have been a useless eyesore without this addition to the facilities.

This provision was to become a regular pattern, experienced over many years. When people came to stay who genuinely required such things as a washing machine or fridge because they were moving into a much-needed flat, those things were offered by people who had no idea at the time that they were needed. Also, time and time again, when more people turned up for a meal at the last moment, there was always enough food to give them. It was just like the miracle of the loaves and fishes.

Another miracle was when a man came from the local rates office. People paid rates in those days, according to the size of the property (these rates have now been replaced by council tax).

'I will claim charity status for this place, so you won't need to pay rates for it,' he told us. We only had charity status through our parish church – but we certainly didn't grumble when he told us this!

So the old house turned into a lovely home. There was a 'blue room', with two single beds in it; and a 'pink room' which was a family room with a double bed and a cot, should it be needed if a baby came to stay. As well as a couple more single rooms and our room at the end of the corridor, there were two single rooms up in the attic, where the boys slept.

The downstairs room, which we used for people who had disabilities or who could not manage stairs, was dubbed 'the nursing room'. However, it was a rule that no-one was made to feel disabled or ill. We had a policy of 'thinking health' all the time. It was a positive house with a positive atmosphere.

Once we were 'up and running', lots of dear ladies came on a regular basis and spent hours in our difficult old kitchen. The lovely results made lots of mouths water! Indeed, the results were delightful. Beautiful cakes appeared as if by magic. They needed to be carefully protected to stop their immediate demise. Vegetables straight from the garden were prepared and cooked – home-grown veg! Yum yum.

How impressed most people must have been to come into a house where a lovely dinner was placed in front of them, day after day, without fail! Breakfast was a casual affair, and so was lunch, although there was always plenty of food to eat. However, dinner was the 'meal of the day'. It fed hungry bodies; it soothed sad souls.

This must have been a new concept to many who had only known deprivation and even squalor before they came to Old Rectory House.

Looking back, perhaps it is fair to say that the main help given to us was all the lovely cooking. How would I have coped without finding gorgeous pies and pasties; roasts ready to cook; vegetables peeled and prepared? All I had to do was to make fun trips to the cash-and-carry, pop the food into the oven and lay up the table. Even that was often done by a kind volunteer.

Just as we were about to sit down to dinner, often unexpected guests would arrive. There was always enough to feed them, too; once again, it was just like the parable of the loaves and fishes!

Of course, none of this could have been achieved without funds, however much kind friends gave us things to keep us going. We were all volunteers, but those of us who were able paid our own way, giving all we had to fund others' needs if necessary – and often that was the case.

We lived by faith, trusting God to supply our needs, but we were not so daft as to think that money came out of thin air. Many sacrifices were quietly made by dear people who made standing orders to support the project. Churches sent regular donations. When bills had to be paid and there wasn't enough money in the bank, someone would come with a gift that just covered the need. How did they know? They didn't. They were people who were listening to the Lord to guide them, and without knowing the need, they gave in obedience to Him. It was often the timing of the gift which was so convincing and so exciting.

After a couple of years our daughter Karen came to live in the house with us, and she gave valuable help, serving up dinners and doing many things which people hardly noticed. But I did – and above all, God did.

Later on, when our son Matt married Jackie, she gave the same wonderful help, which was so gratefully accepted. I would have 'folded' had I not had the help they gave me.

Other dear friends sometimes moved in so that we could get away for a holiday. I still feel very grateful when I think of their help. They're not forgotten.

In the early days at ORH we often experienced financial difficulties. We paid all our living expenses as a family, and provided a car for the work, but we did not think it right to base the project on what would have been a viable business foundation. It was, after all, the Lord's business and we needed to 'live by faith'. This did not mean that we were not responsible with the money. We kept careful account of everything, and had the books and yearly account sheets to prove it. We even provided accounts of our cash spending. If people came to us in trouble, we did not ask them to think about what they should be paying for their board, until they were over their initial upset.

During the first summer at the house, when we were still making decisions about these things, Bryan and I were given a holiday by our friends, Revd John and Margaret Cull, in their beautiful Cotswold rectory.

We were invited to their church on the Sunday, and sat by a dear elderly couple whom we did not know. During the course of conversation, the lady told us that she had been brought up in the 'Muller Homes'. This was a nineteenth- and early twentieth-century Christian orphanage in Bristol, where children were loved and cared for – a sort of 'street children's' project of its day. She began to tell us of her wonderful memories of faith in action at her home, where at times there was nothing, not even food on the table, at which sat many hungry children. When they prayed for their needs they saw God move in miraculous ways, providing bread and other things when they had nothing.

This story seemed to tell us that we should do the same in our project, trusting God for the daily needs there. To put faith into practice in this way was not always easy, although we gained great blessings when our faith was put to the test. We did, indeed, see many miracles, and one or two have come into my mind to share with my readers.

Bryan and I gave our 'everything' to God through this project. We managed with beaten-out old cars (I shared one with our son Andy). We know others who made similar sacrifices. It was a joy to do this, and we knew the blessings which came from it.

One day, burdened with a number of bills, and insufficient money in the bank to pay them, I met Bryan at the Nothe Gardens for a little lunch picnic in his dinner hour. We often met there, as it was a good way to get some time to ourselves away from the pressures of the house. Molly Spiers would be 'holding the fort' for me while I was away.

We held the bills in front of us, as before the Lord, just as Hezekiah did in the Old Testament, and we told Him our concerns. (Read Isaiah 37:14–20.) As we prayed we both knew that we must write the cheques and post them, even though we knew at that moment they would bounce. So we did that and I posted them on my way home.

When I got home, Molly informed me, 'You had a visitor while you were out, Maggie. He left you this envelope.' When I opened it, it contained £50, enough to cover all the cheques we had written to pay the bills! What a wonderful, faithful God we have! It's His perfect timing which often amazes me.

A gentleman, Mr Bob Mills, from St Mary's Church, had felt the Lord was telling him to give some money, and he had obeyed, bringing with him the exact amount we needed to cover all the money we owed. Praise the Lord – and also Mr Mills for his faithfulness. I rushed to the bank, and then wrote to tell

Mr Mills. Later on he gave us a cherry tree for the garden, and every time I passed it I remembered the wonderful miracle.

This and other miracles, great and small, encouraged us very much and built us up in our faith. As time went by, many gifts came for the work. Churches and individuals alike were more than generous, and we felt it had been the right decision to live by faith.

Indeed, there were many other money miracles, when cheques arrived in the post which just covered outstanding needs, and we began to see other sorts of exciting things happening. Often it was the wonderful, perfect timing which impressed us. Sometimes a gift would come in the post, which we found out later was to cover a bill not yet received. People staying in ORH were challenged by this so much that it powerfully confirmed our gospel message, and they soon came to tell us of their new Christian commitment. Both little and big things were happening almost every day!

CHAPTER 10

LOVE IN ACTION

Everyone who came to stay at ORH had a unique story of their own. Some wanted to share their story straight away, but other people hid their story so deep within themselves that it took long hours of prayer and sensitive, gentle talk to encourage them to share anything. Almost all of our guests responded eventually to the love around them.

Sometimes the work of the care centre was misunderstood, because it seemed such a jolly place. However, deep undercurrents hid what was often flowing under the surface. One had to be there and experience the care to understand this. Very often it took time before a guest could open up and share their hurt.

Many of our dear volunteer ladies helped in this ministry. There was Sylvia, a lovely friend who volunteered and stood for long hours 'just ironing' in the kitchen. But in reality she was often listening to someone who was pouring out their hurt, while she silently prayed for them. Many people began to respond to her ministry. At the present time she is 93 years old, well into her old age and riddled with arthritis. I wonder if all that ironing made her so painfully disabled – but I'm sure she doesn't regret all she did.

Many of our guests would start with light topics of conversation and banter. Then they would progress to share what was really on their mind as they told their story, which was often so painful and distressing that both the speaker and the listener would be near to tears.

Dear Sylvia, and others like her, knew when and how to respond. It needed a special sensitivity to know how to help in each situation, and point the person gently to God. She was one of the faithful ladies who sat morning by morning to pray together in the sitting room for anyone or anything needing His attention that day.

This illustrates the whole deep story of Old Rectory House and the Christian care given there. It was, in a nutshell, pure love in action. The volunteers were there when they were needed. No-one was pressurised in any way.

Not everything, of course, was positive and easy. After the house had been running for a while, young people were referred to us by social services. These youngsters could be brash and difficult, and curbs had to be put on bad language or difficult behaviour. We were responsible for the calm atmosphere of the home and had to assert our authority. Sadly, some guests were so deeply embedded in their own sin and bitterness that they didn't, or wouldn't, respond to all the love shown to them, and left us, to continue to cause distress elsewhere. It was just as Jesus said: 'Anyone who blasphemes against the Holy Spirit will not be forgiven' (Luke 12:10).

When we first went to ORH and started the work, we were very naïve. We were trusting of everyone, but there were some people who came to thieve and cause trouble. We lost some valuable items, and I had to set traps to catch the thieves at their sad actions. Once I put some money in a certain place, and watched as one girl came and took it. When challenged she eventually broke down and cried. She told us that she was actually a past colleague's daughter. We phoned her mother, who came and told us such a sad story of events within their family that we were moved to help. The Lord changed their attitudes. So it was worth all the effort of making a challenge about the theft, as in the end it had a happy outcome.

One of the things which we found very difficult to deal with was that many people who came to us were heavy smokers. This I personally found particularly offensive. We had never smoked at home and actually didn't realize how many people did. It was at a time when smoking was still socially acceptable. Things have changed now, but the memory of the smoking still makes me shudder. I still feel, if I have one allergy, it is to cigarette smoke... Ugh!

Most people came to us because of a crisis in their lives. We needed to help them focus on Jesus. We wanted them to learn about Him through the joy which spread through the house and the Christian people who came to minister to them. It was about seeing God's love at first hand. We would hear people say, 'I like it here. There's something lovely about this house.' We knew it was the Holy Spirit who dwelt in it.

These comments from folk made it all worthwhile. A dear friend recently commented, 'Thank God for so many lives changed because of the open home, for so many people, different ages and needs who were all blessed...'

Molly is a friend who lived in an interesting little cottage in Radipole village. It was originally three cottages, but had been made into one in recent times. She was a tower of strength to us (as indeed was Jean, who lived with her family in the house next door).

Molly came every Wednesday to take over the running of the house so that I could have a 'day off'.

One day, when she was working alone, a young man who had come for a short visit told her a very convincing story about his mother, who he said was ill in the Bristol Royal Infirmary. He asked Molly to lend him £60 so that he could go and see her. This was in the early days, when we were still all very naïve, and she believed his story. Sadly, we never saw him again. We were all learning the hard way… but we prayed about it all and the Lord was faithful.

Molly says that one of her vivid memories is about an old lady who came for a holiday. She was a sad, sour, crotchety old soul, with a small downtrodden husband. She was very ill and was nursed in the downstairs bedroom with the help of several dear nurses who came to help look after her. Molly remembers what a job we had to get her false teeth back into her mouth after they had been cleaned! When she was up and dressed, she was helped into a comfy chair by the fire in the main living room. She still grumbled; nothing suited her.

My friend had a real battle to overcome her dislike of this old woman, despite her illness and frailty. She pleaded with the Lord to fill her with His love for the woman, and a miracle occurred for her personally. She started to love her! Molly says she was probably ironing at the time, and talking to her. (So much ministry was done in this way. The dear voluntary ironers were a major part of the ministry in ORH.)

Amazingly, that very night the old lady was rushed off to hospital and died, but something had happened to transform her. She asked someone to read Psalm 23 to her before she slipped away. When my friend Molly saw her, she was completely transformed! Her whole expression had changed. That really was a miracle.

We had wonderful support from our friends who were also neighbours at ORH. We met often to just pray together. We called each other by nicknames. Molly we called 'Joy'; Jean was 'Peace'; and we at ORH were called 'Love'. What happy memories I have! Now I realise that we all had those same attributes – I especially felt joy in my heart as I lived and ministered at ORH. How happy we all were; full of true joy.

CHAPTER 11

THE STORIES OF SOME OF OUR GUESTS

I must tell you the story of my friend Lily. She brought up her three children completely on her own. Her husband spent most of his time in prison. People don't often realise how much the families of prisoners suffer. There is the stigma; the whispers of neighbours and even 'friends' as you pass by, even though the smiles and greetings seem genuine enough.

When Lily came for her first 'holiday' with the children, she was very depressed, and we did what we could to soothe her. I took her back to her home when the time came for her to leave us. I helped her sort out her house and get enough provisions to keep them all going. I remember sleeping (in my sleeping bag) on her settee that night. The next morning, we went for a walk together before I came home. She lived in a beautiful part of Wiltshire, but it was very isolated.

More visits to ORH were arranged, and the next time she came she brought a couple of dogs as well as the children! Her little boy had his sixth birthday party in the garden. We carried the dining table outside on to the lawn. It was a very happy event. So Lily and her family were all feeling very much better. Lily had coped well after her first visit. She was a very intelligent lady and started to realise her potential. She also had made some very good friends where she lived (who had sent her on her first holiday with us), who helped and supported her, even finding her better accommodation. Lily and I have remained good friends and we meet up as often as possible. We always enjoy a trip to Portland Bill – the fish and chips are lovely at the café there!

I wonder what happened to the lad called Aidan? He was a 16-year-old boy from a terribly dysfunctional family. Bryan had cause to visit his home when he was working for the council's housing department. He saw a framed picture of Hitler on the wall! Later, Aidan told us that his mother was a spiritualist medium.

I remember one occasion when I asked him to rescue a child visitor who had locked himself in the loo. Instantly Aidan found a knife and with a quick flick the door was opened! I also remember when he joined a party of us who went to Poole, in order to hear David Pawson, a world-renowned speaker, lead a seminar. Aidan was very restless and disappeared during the interval. We later learned that he had stolen a car from the car park and driven it all the way home. (He was only 16 and Poole was a long way away.) He continued to drive it around Weymouth for several days before the police caught him.

I went to the magistrates' court a couple of times with him. I testified that he was always kind and good to me, personally, at home. But, oh dear, I found out that he was a terror when he was away from us!

Aidan had a girlfriend who, although she was very pretty, had a strange look about her and for some unknown reason made me feel uncomfortable. Aidan boasted to me one day, as he sat in the kitchen with his arm around her, 'Her mother's been selling her to the sailors since she was 11.' (The navy was based in Portland Harbour at the time.) I just couldn't believe that comment. However, given all the shocking talk about immorality everywhere in the 1970s, I wonder if that was indeed true.

Poor young Aidan was a thief. A lovely lady came all the way from Poole on the bus to help with the chores. Being so trusting, she left her handbag wide open on a chair. Aidan must have taken her keys and purse out of it and hidden them somewhere. After this dear lady realised they were missing, he was actually to be seen comforting her and trying to help her find them, all the time knowing what he had done. What distress for her that day! She had to ask the police to help her get into her house, and arrange for new keys to be cut so that the thief would not be able to get in. Sadly, we never saw her again. It worried me for a long time. Eventually we found out what Aidan had done, but it was too late then to make amends.

The Revd Johnson stayed a night with us before he preached at St John's Church, Weymouth. I must tell you about his visit. He was a famous itinerant preacher. We gave him the best bedroom, as he was special and we wanted to honour him as much as we could.

We had forgotten about the cat! Our cat, Purkiss (for a purr and a kiss), had an important job to do at ORH as the many mice had to be kept at bay. However, he did have a few habits which were embarrassing. He would silently disappear under the bed of the most recent visitor, and wake up in the early hours of the morning when our new friend was fast asleep. He then would walk all over the unsuspecting person until they woke up. He really enjoyed this game, as they usually screamed in fright. It was an understandable reaction, and the cat loved it! Poor Mr Johnson.

He reacted as most people did, and couldn't get to sleep again. So, in the end, he decided to get up. He went to the bathroom to shave, and found the tap running cold. At the time we had a rather troubled girl staying with us, and she used to get up in the night and turn on the taps all over the house. Oh poor, poor Mr Johnson.

Our turn for embarrassment came when we were all at St John's, listening to him preach. He told the congregation all about the terrible house where he had had such dreadful experiences!

CHAPTER 12

THE ABUNDANT, CRAZY, BUSY LIFE OF A HOUSE OF PEACE

How happy we all were at ORH, and what fun we had! Every day something happened to make us laugh, and filled us with a wonderful joy. Talk about the abundant life… we were living it.

This is an extract from a letter sent by a young friend who lived next door to us, in which she reminisces about those days. It's good to have her objective view.

> We moved next door to ORH when I was about 13. We used to trip across the little patch of wasteland garden to their back door. Dad had made a bridge across the little stream – unfortunately he had made it out of the lovingly carved tombstone of a long-lost dog: 'Fern, deeply missed'! We were all horrified, and never trod on it out of respect, but our dad, as ever, was making practical use of something without thinking of the emotional effect on the early teenagers who had to cross it.

The back door always seemed to be open. This led into a medium-sized kitchen with a big Aga. There was usually some parish woman in the kitchen. The living room was full of photos of the Dukes' children, so obviously central to the whole house. We then went through the house to the driveway to find Bryan waiting for us, as he gave us all a lift to the grammar school. (We probably made him late for work so many times.) He was always nice to us and I remember he had a distinctive Weymouth accent and used the word 'see' a lot, as they do in South Wales. My sister, Cathy, who was about 17, sat in the back, and Matt, who was about 15 or 16, sat in the front with Bryan, who was always winding down the window and berating Matt for farting in the car… which we thought hilarious (as our parents never commented on things like that); but now that I'm older, I think it may not have been poor Matt *every* time!

I remember that there were always lots of teenagers, older and more exotic than me, at ORH, and there was always something dramatic happening. One of the first people I can remember was a young man who had a head injury, and used to want to play cards (which were the size of shoeboxes) with you. I also remember a rather Bohemian woman (from Australia, with an amazing story of her own) who was pregnant. Mum and Maggie were thinking that they might have to act as midwives, as she was wanting a home birth… *Bad idea*, I remember thinking. Luckily she went into hospital, I think.

I remember Aidan and his dubious skills that came in handy if you had locked yourself out of the house!

I remember the apiarists visiting, and the rectory bees swarmed into our garden. When we saw the summer sky filled with moving black dots, Debbie, our housemate, and I thought it was the end of the world (we watched too many horror films!); but it was fascinating to watch the bees swarming over each other.

> When I was a bit older I made friends with some of the many visitors. I went to secretarial college with a girl (whose name I can't remember). [Insert by Maggie: I think this must have been Janie.] She was brilliant at shorthand and typing, and put all the rest of us to shame. I met my amazing, whacky friend, Freda, at ORH – a hairdresser from Dundee [the same lady who turned all the taps on at night]. We had a lot of fun together, and hitch-hiked back to her home once. She used to remember her time at ORH for years afterwards.
>
> They were happy days, Maggie, and we cherished having such lovely neighbours, so full of life and living. I remember Karen and Paul's Helen, when she was only about 3. (She'll hate this!) She had wandered from your garden into the paddock, then into our garden. I got some toys for her to play with; then I thought I'd better take her back, especially when I realised she wasn't wearing any knickers! Free spirit! [This little girl is now a happily married woman, with a daughter of that age herself.]

Sometimes in our mixed household horrible problems would occur. It was not always joy and light. There was an incident one dinnertime which shocked everyone around the table. After this, the young people took their plates into the sitting room to eat separately from the adults, just in case it happened again – but in fact it never did.

A dear old man came to have a little holiday with us, but he was really too old to cope. His daughter was a friend whom I had met in the hospital, and she had begged me to take him, even for a few days. His name was Simon, and he had been a lighthouse keeper for many years.

As he sat at the table, he began to cough, and out popped his false teeth into the roast potatoes! Then he began to vomit. As I started to help him get up to go to the toilet, he began to be grossly incontinent. It went all down his trousers and on to the carpet. As I led him from the room, there was a trail of faeces all the way through the hall and into the downstairs toilet. Where to start cleaning up? Of course, I was a nurse and so had seen it all before, but almost no-one else around the table had, and they found it very shocking. I don't think anyone ate their dinner that night. This was the sort of problem that could occur when you looked after all sorts of people in all conditions, and one we needed God's grace to cope with.

The principle and vision of ORH was that it must show God's love to the world around it in a practical way (John 3:16). Just to 'be there' for people was enough. That is what it stood for, more than the work which was actually done within the walls. It had to be a witness to our Lord and Master. We tried to do something positive about a world situation that was, and still is, far bigger than we have power to influence, but about which we can do our little 'something'. As Mother Teresa said, 'There's an ocean of need, but the ocean is made up of little drops.'

So the house was made available for anyone in any sort of need. We wanted to confirm the worship of our churches, and aim to bring people into the life which Jesus gives through them. We always tried to support our church in every way we could, and brought everyone who stayed in the house to the family service each Sunday while they were with us. We also tried to give priority to requests from our own clergy and congregation, but this was not always possible if the house was already full.

Of course, we needed that small army of volunteers who willingly came to help and keep the house in a welcoming state. Every morning a little group – whoever was helping at the house that day – met in the quiet sitting room to pray for the people who were staying with us and others for whom we had particular concerns. We asked the Lord to send only the people of His choice, and keep others away.

We made many mistakes, of course, but I do remember someone telling me that anyone who never made a mistake never made anything!

On Saturday mornings, very early, around 7 a.m. winter and summer, a group mainly of men, but with a few women as well, went to St Ann's Church to pray for the work. Prayer was the mainstay at ORH. Nothing of value would have been achieved without it.

As time went by, we were asked to have groups for discussions about Christian topics, held in the sitting room; also parties in the garden and even wedding receptions! Many local churches were involved together in these events, and this brought many local Christian people to know and understand each other better.

We were also the recipients of many gifts from churches and individuals, which often came in miraculous ways. Our lives were full and happy, and enriched beyond measure, growing to love people whom we soon began to look upon as our own family, while still acknowledging their own families and encouraging their healthy relationships at the same time.

CHAPTER 13

MORE SPECIAL PEOPLE AND SPECIAL MIRACLES

Martin was a very special volunteer who rescued the garden. The large garden was nearly 3 acres of fine alluvial soil, and contained a big vegetable plot. It became a real challenge to take care of this because very few people were free to come and help tend it during the week. Bryan, who loved gardening, would gladly have spent all his time out there, but he had to go to work. So we prayed, and along came Martin. Our Roman Catholic friend who was coming as a volunteer asked us if Martin could come and dig the garden.

'Don't try to engage him in conversation or involve him in the things happening in the house,' we were told. 'You'll send him away if you do.' So we took the advice and left him alone.

Martin was a very quiet and thoughtful man. He was a devout Christian, rather retiring, but became a faithful friend. We didn't get to know him until he had been coming to dig the vegetable patch for some time. Then gradually, as cups of coffee were taken down to him, and the children staying in the house started talking to him whenever they saw him, calling him 'Uncle Mart', he began of his own accord to come into the house and get to know people. Gradually, as the year progressed, a beautiful garden began to appear. Vegetables of every kind were growing there, food for the hungry folk who ate everything offered at the table.

The garden thrived under Martin's clever touch. As time went by, he came to need accommodation and moved into the attic. It became his special domain. He was always a joy to have around – a real gentleman, very deeply spiritual and sensitive.

I remember how lovely the garden was when Martin tended it. Two greenhouses had been donated, which stood by the vegetable patch, and they were full of beautiful tomatoes and cucumbers in the summer. One year he grew sunflowers which were about 17 feet high. I loved to escape to the garden and help him prick out the little seedlings to grow into bigger plants.

I remember too that, longing for a little time to myself, I always tried to be the one to peg out the washing on the two big lines which were in that part of the garden. One day, there was no-one there, and it being a very stressful day, I lay down behind a row of tall plants Martin had grown, which made a good hiding place. Martin found out about this, and made me a 'secret garden' behind a fence with a knot pushed out in one place so that if anyone came up the drive I was able to see who the visitor was. This quiet place was a real solace to me. Since then, I have cultivated my own back garden to resemble it.

As time went by, the government of the day decided to create a 'Manpower Services Scheme'. Martin became the leader of a small group of men who had been unable to get work for some time. The plan was intended to encourage them to gain the daily discipline that an employer would require before they could get and keep a job.

This was wonderful for both Martin and the garden. Each man employed was given a grant of £400 per year for any equipment required to help them in their chosen work. So in this way some really good tools were added to the old ones Martin had coped with up until then. The garden was soon transformed into a place of beautiful colour and fruitfulness. It was truly a delight to be in. Soon we had a waiting list of church groups and people who wanted to come for picnics and parties. An old gentleman who came to stay with us for a rest after many years of sacrificial ministry commented that the garden was just like heaven to him. On a spring morning, one could really imagine it could be just that.

Here's a story which *must* be told! One day, Jean and I were in the main visitors' family bedroom, making the bed, when we both pulled a bit too hard and the sheet tore down the middle.

'Oh dear!' I exclaimed. 'We don't have another suitable sheet. In fact, all of them are getting too old and frail to use. What shall we do?'

'Pray for some more,' answered Jean, and immediately began to pray. Being a little less trusting of this approach to the Almighty, I added, 'Please could we have some coloured ones as I'm fed up with these white ones.' (Wicked woman!)

We were interrupted by the ringing of the front doorbell. This was rather unusual because most visitors just walked in. I went downstairs to open the door. On the step stood a lady whom I didn't know.

'I wonder if you could use this bedding?' she said. 'We have to find a home for it, as we're clearing out a house because our mother has to go into a residential home.'

There were several big bags of sheets, candy-striped and other colours. Also there were useful blankets and counterpanes.

Oh glory! It was the perfect timing, as much as the gifts themselves, which just 'blew me away'.

This was a truly amazing event – a miracle – and events like this occurred time and time again.

CHAPTER 14

NURSING THE SICK

The end of one summer school term arrived, and with it, a new visitor. Matt brought a school friend home, whom we hardly knew. The boys disappeared quickly up into the attic, without so much as a glance at any of us in the kitchen. Later, Matt came down, saying his friend wanted to have his dinner up there. This new addition to the family had refused to leave the attic and eat with everyone else.

The next thing was, 'Mum, Paul says "Is there anything else left to eat?" He's still hungry!'

I heard our 14-year-old son running down the stairs, two at a time. His friend had sent him yet again with another hunger message. I put the almost empty cooking dish of 'Queen's Pudding' on the tray that Matt was holding, and told him that a scraping around the edge was the very last bit left!

There had been about sixteen people around the table that night for dinner. We provided only simple food, but it was always filling and acceptable to most tastes. The house was a hive of activity. This new friend was an extra person squeezed into a house already bursting at the seams.

As well as our own family, a motley group of people were staying in the house. A young African single mother, sent by a London City Missionary, was having a week's holiday with her 2-year-old son. Neither of them was at all domesticated, and the child was difficult to restrain, as his mother did nothing to stop him doing whatever he wanted.

Also, the large dining room had for that week been turned into a nursing room, with a hospital bed and a hoist for a profoundly disabled 18-stone guest. His wife occupied the adjoining room, and spent all her waking time with her husband.

A small group of volunteer helpers, most of them with nursing experience, were coming day by day to help with the specialised care required for this gentleman. In this way, his wife could be relieved for a while from the heavy burden of looking after him, and enjoy a little holiday herself in this haven of peace and rest. While they were with us they could forget about their problems and pretend they were young folk again, having a quiet holiday in the country.

Peace and rest? The scene which I have just described didn't sound quite like that!

Quiet holiday? The house could be noisy, but strangely it did also seem to be a quiet place at the same time. In the midst of so many happenings and so many different people coming and going, this is what the place was – a haven of peace and rest, quiet and relaxing.

I had first met Nigel and Alice when I worked as a district nurse. I had been very impressed with them because I saw a valiant struggle going on to overcome insurmountable problems. For years Nigel had been getting more and more stiff and immobile. At the time when they visited he was completely paralysed and unable to speak, but always had a brave smile. At home they had a hospital bed in their living room, and a hoist to lift him when we had to do the required nursing care. Alice looked after him faithfully, and when I went there to help her she was always so cheerful and made little remarks to reassure Nigel that she was coping well. However, she would slip into the kitchen where I would find her silently crying her eyes out. We would hug each other to try to relieve her pain.

By the time that the work of ORH was well established, Nigel was in long-term hospital care. Alice had to accept that she just couldn't cope at home any more. It was heart-breaking.

Then we realised that we could do something for them. We arranged with the hospital that the necessary equipment be borrowed from the central hospital store, and it was delivered to grace our dining room! It nearly filled that big room. The day arrived when the ambulance team brought Nigel and settled him in the bed. He was an 18-stone man, and his limbs were as stiff as a board; he was unable to sit or bend. How were we going to cope? By God's grace, we did. It was a miracle. For two wonderful weeks, Alice and I managed the hoist, washed and cared for Nigel, and made fun and jokes all the time! We were so happy. Many lovely nurse friends just 'turned up' to help, so in fact no-one became too tired.

It was winter and I have a touching memory of the dog and cat stretched out in luxury, side by side on the mat in front of the open fire, while Alice knitted away as she sat in the armchair, and Nigel watched them in that particular way he had which made one think he was choked with joy.

At the end of that first holiday another ambulance team came to take Nigel back to the hospital. They looked at him and firmly stated that there was no way they were going to lift him, even with hoists and help. Yet Alice and I had been doing it for two weeks with no ill effects! Although we told them this, they insisted on sending for another ambulance team to help them.

These dear people came for several lovely holidays after that first one. The last time they came it was in May and exceptionally beautiful weather. Every day, after the care was done, six strong young men, three each side, lifted Nigel in his hospital bed through the French windows and down three steps on to the lawn. He was wheeled to the far side of the lawn to spend his days in the shade under the trees, watching the old house and all the activities within. A special airbed was needed to nurse him, and all the electric extension leads in the house were strung together to reach from the plug nearest the door to the end of the bed. Chairs were taken out, and the big dining table. (I still have that in my present house. It is a very valued possession.)

Nigel and Alice's daughters and their families came to visit, and the whole family were able to have a private party together in the sunshine.

Before Nigel returned to hospital after that visit, Alice asked if he could have a little worship service. Revd John Robinson, who was then the vicar of Emmanuel Church, kindly came to minister to him, and held a simple communion with just the three of us there. When we prayed the Lord's Prayer, John and I were amazed to hear Nigel repeat every word distinctly, even though he had not uttered a word for years!

Ten days after he returned to hospital, this gallant soul suffered a heart attack and went to be with his Lord. He was ready to go. How glad and privileged we were to have been part of his story, and to have been able to help this valiant couple.

During the early days at ORH we had a number of disabled and sick people who came to stay at the house for a holiday, with their husband/wife carer. We were always able to borrow a hospital bed for those who needed it, and sometimes even a hoist or other equipment to use during their stay. Most of these people were former patients of mine when I had been a sister on the district.

The little room which previously had been the rector's study now became the nursing room for anyone too frail to manage the stairs. It was not ideal, as it was just inside the front door and often a bit noisy, and there were no en-suite facilities such as are taken for granted these days.

Sometimes we had terminally ill people come for a bit of special care, or to give their carer a much-needed rest. Once or twice a visitor became so ill that they had to be admitted to hospital as an emergency. We had our GP friend to support us, so if there was a real problem he was only a phone call away. But there were times when the stress was truly great. Some visitors were very old and frail, and became incontinent and distressingly confused and incapable. We did prove, however, that God is good and He never allowed the stresses to become overwhelming.

Even in tragic circumstances, there was always something to smile about, such as when one couple came to stay: Kitty and her husband. Kitty was a very poorly little lady. Quite soon after she had gone happily home after her little 'holiday', she was taken very ill and died, so we were all glad that she had been so happy at ORH.

Sometime later, Kitty's husband sent us a letter to express his gratitude for the holiday, which they had so much enjoyed together. He wanted to give us a present. He explained that, as he had been a furrier in the happy days before his retirement and Kitty's illness, he wanted to donate some of the precious (to him) furs he owned. How could we refuse, when the gift was so well meant and so lovingly given?

One afternoon the furs arrived in a big box. We were rather nonplussed as to what to do with them, so they were put on one side until we made up our minds.

Some of the boys had a bright idea. They took a fox fur, with the head stuffed and intact – the sort of fur that was the trendy thing for a lady to wear round her shoulders in the 1930s – and they put it on Karen's bedding and pillows while she was at work. When she came home and went to her room, there was the fox, looking very lifelike in the fading light! The window was open as it had been a lovely summer's day, so she thought an animal had come in. She gave it one look, and rushed downstairs in panic. How the boys laughed! They were always playing practical jokes.

Karen has never forgotten this incident – I think it really frightened her at the time.

1.The Body of Christ in action – Painters

2. Gardeners

3. Jean ironing

4. Mike gardening

5. God's amazing provision – Volunteers

6. Volunteers

7. Volunteers

8. God's amazing provision – Round the table

9a. Harry and Gwen's wedding

9b. Louise and Molly at Harry and Gwen's wedding

9c. Harry and Gwen's wedding helpers

10. Some of the many people we were privilidged to love

11.

12.

13.

14.

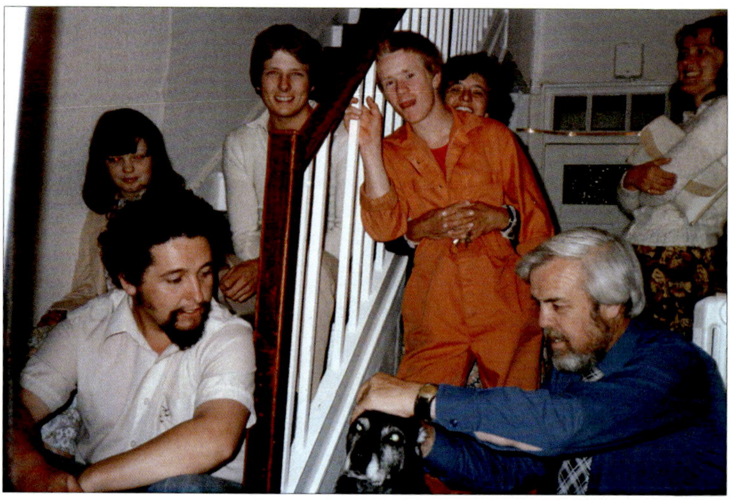

15.

16.

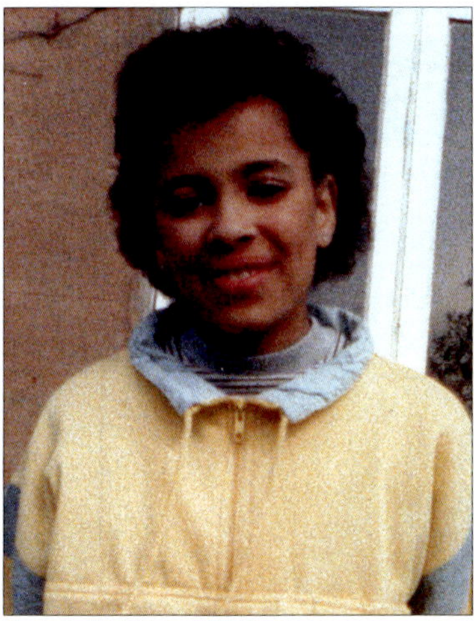

17. Gen

18. Neil and Jacky

19.

20. Jerry and Tom

21. Joyce

CHAPTER 15

STORIES OF THE YOUNG PEOPLE AND FOSTER CHILDREN

After being at Old Rectory House for just a short while, our teenage children started to tell us about their peers who were asking to be helped. At first, our youngsters were being misunderstood, labelled 'religious weirdos', but soon they were being asked for help.

We all became increasingly aware of the suffering among so many youngsters, who found it hard to share their problems with older people but would feel understood by people their own age. Before long we were taking in teenage foster children. The attic rooms were turned into 'Boy Land'. When I think back now, I wonder how we coped, with sick people downstairs, and boys full of fun and mischief in the attic. Well, not just the attic, but all over the house, the garden – and sometimes even the town! It would have been chaos had not the Holy Spirit been in control. Was God laughing, too? We certainly were. It made me think of Psalm 133: 'How good and pleasant it is when brothers live together in unity!' Most of these young folk had grown up in very sad homes. It was a new experience for them to live in a home where people loved each other; laughed and sang together; were patient with each other. They soon began to respond, and thrived in such an atmosphere.

One of our lovely foster boys had a friend called Tom, who had been injured in a car crash. He needed a wheelchair in order to get around. The boys called themselves 'Tom and Jerry' after the cat and mouse cartoon duo which was being shown on the TV at the time. This was because Tom in the wheelchair really was 'Tom', and 'Jerry' truly his friend.

Tom could perform spectacular 'wheelies' in his chair, and even played tennis sitting in it.

We took the boys to church services, and they responded happily to all the teaching. It was truly a wonderful church where such colourful, often socially unacceptable boys were welcomed to the services. Tom had a 'Mohican' hairstyle, and both boys wore the trappings of the 'punk' lifestyle.

It was, however, obvious that Tom was really very frail. One evening, Jerry went to his flat and found him dead in bed. We were not sure of the cause of his death, but of course Jerry was terribly upset.

Tom's funeral was crowded with young people. Most of them were dressed as punks, but they were listening carefully and responding to the Holy Spirit. It made me think of how Jesus accepted sinners and loved them all. He loves and understands each one of us. These young people are all middle-aged men and women now. They are responsible members of the community, good family-orientated people. Jerry is still a much-loved friend; a successful businessman and a loving husband, father and grandfather. He's a very special person. I saw him talking very happily to my son Matt at a skittle party we had recently. What a darling! Two darling men.

We took in our first foster son at the end of the school term, July 1977. Matt just arrived home with a mystery lad behind him. He was the starving lad, Paul, whom I wrote about earlier. When the boys arrived home that afternoon, I had such a houseful, and the little African boy from London was with me in the kitchen, so I had no opportunity to meet this first of our foster sons until much later. However, I do remember that moment distinctly: I was sure the Lord was telling me that he would preach in Jesus' Name one day! This was a true word of prophecy, for now he often preaches powerfully in the local churches – in fact he preached at St Ann's Church the Sunday previous to my writing this.

At the beginning of Paul's stay it was very difficult. Paul disappeared, staying up in the attic bedroom – only coming down to the bathroom when no-one was about. Every mealtime he asked Matt to go to the kitchen and collect his food. We could get no response from him at all. After about a fortnight of this behaviour, Bryan told me to go up and tell Paul that he was coming out with us and should put on decent clothes (not that he had any!).

A silent Paul met us outside and we took him for a drive through some of the local countryside. It was a silent trip. At last we arrived at a local inn, the Elm Tree pub, and saw that the garden was almost deserted since it was starting to get dark. Paul and I sat at a table while Bryan went in to buy some crisps and drinks. After a few more minutes of silence, Paul suddenly started to talk.

'I think my mother will go to prison this time,' he said.

(She never did, to my knowledge. I think she was too clever for that.)

Once Paul started talking, he couldn't stop. He went on telling us a long, sad tale until all the lights had gone out and the pub was shut. In shock – for it was the first time we had heard a tale like this – we drove home and all went to bed. The next morning I looked out of the bedroom window and there was Paul, skipping across the lawn with the dog! For Paul, it was the start of a wonderful revival of his youth.

He was a challenging boy in many ways, but such fun. He could be very cheeky and even rude at times. I remember one time when we were throwing the dishcloth at each other from one end of the kitchen to the other. (Who relived her childhood then?!) I soon became very fond of Paul – and I still am, for he is my beloved son-in-law, the grandfather of little Millie and Olivia, and a devoted Christian family man who takes an active part in church life.

CHAPTER 16

BOYS WILL BE BOYS!

One afternoon I was all alone in the house, and this was a very rare occurrence. A knock came at the front door. This, too, was strange, as most people either came straight in or looked for the 'key in the tree' (everyone who knew the house usually found this out in the first day or two).

I answered the door to find a very 'cleric'-looking gentleman standing there, in black clothes and gaiters! He explained in an ecclesiastical sort of voice that he had heard something of the work in which we were involved, and since he was visiting the area, he thought he would come and find out more.

I invited him in and sat him down with a cup of tea while I showed him some of the current photographs and answered his questions. Afterwards I asked him if he would like to see the house. We walked all round, eventually reaching the attic where the boys lived. As I climbed the stairs I remembered with foreboding that I had heard them talking among themselves recently about marrow rum! They had decided to make some with one of the vegetable marrows, which grew to a huge size in our prolific garden. They had taken out the seeds from the middle and filled it with demerara sugar, purchased from the shop over the hill. They had then hung the marrow up in an old pair of tights pinched from one of the girls. I could smell this at the bottom of the stairs, and as we mounted higher, so the aroma became stronger and stronger, until the stink was overpowering. I didn't know what to do about it, as I guessed that my visitor had very little sense of humour and most probably disapproved of strong drink. We went into the boys' room, and I stood in front of the offending bag of marrow, which was hanging from the rafters. I hoped he wouldn't notice – but then, I took a fatal mistaken step backwards, and my back touched the marrow in the tights, whereupon it burst with a slurp, and poured its contents into a basin, which had been placed underneath it to catch the rum. The smell was overpowering and my embarrassment complete. The gentleman couldn't get out of the house quickly enough. I wonder if he told his friends about this terrible house where they took people 'in', but it was really a distillery in disguise!

On another occasion, as one of my faithful helpers, Sylvia, and I made up one of the boys' beds with clean linen, we turned the mattress for him. There, hidden underneath, was an empty 'Durex' packet. I kept it as evidence, and tackled the offender about it that evening when he came home. After that the girls were *strictly forbidden* to visit the attic.

It didn't totally solve my problems as a few of the girls were determined to flout the rules. The story has a happy ending, because in time this particular couple, who were the culprits, became responsible Christians, giving up their immorality. After they had grown older they married and today live very happy and fulfilled lives with their own growing family. I am sure they carry on the teaching which they learned through this experience. My own fears of handing out 'tough love' were unfounded and it was the best thing that could have happened, although at the time I was quite upset about it.

(I feel very sad for young people in these twenty-first-century 'enlightened times', when all sorts of immoral activities are accepted as the norm. I wonder what lasting damage we are doing to the next generation by allowing so many temptations to invade their lives.)

Bryan and I were offered a couple of weeks' holiday in our friends' lovely rectory in the Cotswolds while they were away. After a very stressful initial six months at ORH we were really in need of a rest. It happened to be over the time of Matt's fifteenth birthday, but, perhaps in retrospect a little too keenly, the children said they would cope with the party and do everything. All we needed to do was to provide the cash. If we had known what they were planning, I doubt that we could have slept in our beds so soundly. I remember we came home to find a very peaceful, calm house, but we wondered what was stuck in the rose bush under the dining room window. It was a pair of underpants!

Apparently, there had been a lot of 'goings on' with unruly teenagers and some drinks. The boys had climbed out of the attic dormer windows and been sitting on the roof smoking cigarettes! Thankfully, drug taking was almost completely unknown in those days. That was the night that Karen first met her mate in the form of Paul: only 15 himself at the time, leaning over a tree trunk that lay at the bottom of the garden and being violently sick. (My comment would have been 'Serves him right!')

However, no real and lasting harm came from this event, and now they are all happy, responsible people and really good role models for the youngsters of today.

Matt and his wife, Jackie, cope cheerfully with big family responsibilities as well as those at church.

Karen and Paul help run a youth group in the church, lead youth services, and take an active part in preaching and in the music. Who could have dreamed that such a poor beginning would have turned out so well? It's amazing what God can do!

Of course, I have two other adult 'children'; they, too, are involved in wonderful caring professions. Sally is a nurse at the local hospital, and our eldest son, Andrew, teaches at a college in Yeovil for young adults with disabilities, and is well known for his wise and caring attitude.

CHAPTER 17

MORE BOYS

It was a busy morning, with the house full of visitors and noise. When the phone rang I answered it a little impatiently.

'Yes?' I said, recognising the voice on the other end with a sinking heart.

'Margaret,' he said, 'I have a young man here who needs you to give him a home.' David was an old school friend of Bryan and was now the rector of St Paul's Church, a couple of miles away across the town. 'Please, Maggie, will you find a place for a lad we have here who desperately needs a home?'

'I can't, David,' I answered, 'because we're overloaded with people at the moment, and there just isn't a space to put him. Sorry…'

'For old time's sake, please find a spot' was the reply. 'This is a very genuine case, and we've been very concerned about him for a long time at the church.'

'Bring him over, then,' I responded. 'He may have to sleep on the floor.'

This was typical of the pressure we were under – often obliged to break the law to make room for urgent cases.

Neil arrived on that bleak November morning. He had been sleeping on the beach for several nights. He came from a local family who had a very sad history. We found out much later that his grandfather was a dear Christian man who had been a lay preacher in his younger days, but Neil didn't seem to know him at the time. (Subsequently, the grandfather himself came to have a little holiday with us, and had a lovely time. He died only a couple of weeks after that visit, so we were so glad of that happy time with him.)

Neil's mother had left home in desperation. She left no forwarding address, and Neil didn't know how to find her. He had looked after his father for some time, although he was only 17 years old. His father had caused much of the distress and at this time had become impossible to please. Neil left, or was thrown out.

His former teacher, David Green, who was now the priest of the local church, just begged me to take him in. I didn't want to, as I have just recorded, as I had a house full of people already and my experience with Paul made me feel that I couldn't cope with another teenage boy. (I was to be proved so wrong as so many teenage boys came through our door over the years.)

Neil arrived and stood at the kitchen door. He had a cross earring in his ear, and a jumper with a pattern of distorted Christian symbols on the front. I remember thinking, *Ugh! I don't want this one here!*

I gave him the little room just inside the front door, so that I could keep as good an eye on him as possible. It was intended for elderly or disabled people, but it was the only space, and even that was booked for someone to come the next day. There were certain advantages in putting Neil there because he had no reason to venture up the stairs to the rest of the house. Within a few days, though, Matt came to me and asked if he could invite Neil to share his room in the attic, just as Paul had done when he stayed with us. I remember cautioning Matt about him. 'He's two years older than you, Matt,' I said. 'He'll try to corrupt you.'

(As I sit and write this, thirty years later, they – Paul, Neil and Matt – along with their wives, Karen, Jacky and Jackie, are meeting together for supper and an evening of prayer. How wonderful is that? 'It is the Lord's doing and marvellous in our eyes!')

Neil had a steady girlfriend, called Jacky. She is now his adored wife and they have four lovely children, growing up into fine young adults. However, when Neil first came it was a very different story. He sat in the best chair. (All the youngsters sat in the best chair if it became empty even for a moment. It was Bryan's chair, and I always felt very jealous about it for him, but he never minded and only sat down first thing in the day to read his Bible and pray, or when he came in very tired after work.)

'So, you're all Christians here, I'm told,' Neil said. 'I'll join. How much are the subs?' Cynicism didn't become him…

It was a whole year before Neil gave his life to the Lord. It happened one amazing evening. Jacky, his girlfriend, had told me that she couldn't resist Jesus any longer, her face shining with such a light that I still have a thrill as I remember it. Neil sat on the garden seat opposite the house and was in a bad mood. He never has bad moods now – and I still have that garden seat in my tiny garden. He had such a fight to come to terms with the Lord's calling that it made me think of Jacob when he wrestled with the angel. It was the end of the evening, I think around eleven o'clock, with all the stars shining and the moon the only light, before he conceded. But the Light of God was switched on in Neil as he gave his life to Him. What a wonderful moment!

Neil changed overnight, and he has never looked back. He found his mother, and he and Jacky were very good to her until her death. His dad went to hospital with Alzheimer's disease. Neil and Jacky, although such busy people, regularly took him out for coffee on a Saturday morning, and both of them were very caring and kind to him.

Now, as I continue to write the story, Neil is working as the community chaplain in Portland, and preaches regularly at St Aldhelm's and St Ann's, two churches in Radipole, on Sundays. They are a happy, vibrant, generous couple, who are one of the many delights of my heart.

One day, a social worker was on the phone. 'Could you give a 14-year-old boy a home during the school holidays? He's at a boarding school a few miles away. He's been there since he came out of hospital, having sustained head and chest injuries at home from a stepfather, so he won't be going home again.'

I arrived a minute or so late at the bus station, and there Ian was. My heart missed a beat! Such a sad little figure with bright ginger hair stuck straight up on top, and with a little old-fashioned suitcase by his side, looking the picture of misery.

It took a few days for Ian to adjust. Our dog was the one to help him at first, and we saw Ian running across the lawn with him, just as we had seen other youngsters before him. What a blessing that dog was! Zeta was a Labrador cross – possibly with a greyhound – and she had a wonderful ministry all of her own, healing hurting people, and Ian was certainly one of them.

Where was the terrible monster we had been led to believe we were going to have staying with us? True, there were major problems which we didn't at first see, but we all fell in love with Ian. He was the most engaging and delightful little chap, and proved to be very talented. He was such a natural comic and very musical. Often he had us all in fits of laughter with his sudden, inspirational dressing-up stunts and ideas for fun. He brought a whole new lightness to the household. I have photographs of him pretending to cut up the bread with a chainsaw! Once he came silently into the dining room, wearing a huge boiler suit, gloves on his feet and a big monkey mask over his face. He could have had a career in the entertainment world if opportunities had been opened to him. Some of the fun he brought will stay with us forever. One time we were wondering what to have for tea as there wasn't much food that day, when he announced, 'Let's have bean on crumb!' It had us all in fits of laughter. When Ian was happy, we were all happy!

One evening Neil heard Ian talking with Matt and plotting to have a midnight feast in the little caravan we had in the garden. Neil told me that he had a big, black, furry spider on a long black string. He suggested that we go out when they were cooking up their feast and silently drop it through the little roof skylight to give them a fright.

'What a good idea!' I said, and so, when it was dark, and they were enjoying their little escapade, we got the metal stepladder, opened it up and crept into the garden. The idea was that I should hold the steps while Neil climbed up and put the spider through the skylight.

However, as soon as we started to carry the steps, they creaked. We heard one of the boys say, 'Did you hear something?' Of course, we started to laugh and had a job trying to hold in our giggles. After a minute we crept a bit further, but the giggles were a problem… As Neil reached the top of the steps, he just choked, and the boys knew we were there, and came out of the caravan, laughing and shouting at us in glee! Before they had their midnight feast, we all rolled around on the grass, helpless with laughter. What fun we had! It was one bit of fun after another. Life was so sweet. People who came in tears were so happy to find something to laugh about. They realised that Jesus' love is full of joy and fun.

(This was the essence of Old Rectory House. How mistaken people are to think that church is all gloom and doom. It's the very opposite!)

Another example of the fun we had is this story. One year, Bryan's birthday fell on the Sunday before Christmas. After the New Year, he was going to start working in Portland. So, as I was very concerned about it being so cold there in the winter, I bought him some thermal long johns, and a top like a T-shirt, with sleeves down to the elbow. They were a bright, French navy colour.

We all had dinner and then went to relax in the sitting room at the end of the corridor behind the dining room, while Bryan, being Bryan, finished all the washing up and clearing away in the kitchen, on his own. Suddenly, the door opened and a 'ballet dancer' appeared, doing funny pirouettes, wearing his new thermals! We were all laughing so loudly that no-one heard the front door ringing. As the key was always in the door, the people at the door – kind people whom we didn't know – came in. There were three or four people, all dressed in formal dark coats and large brimmed hats, looking rather stern. They had come from St Nicholas' Church in the next parish. At their morning service they had a special gift day for the poor children living at ORH, and had brought some boxes of gifts to give out. They just walked into the room. Poor Bryan, who was well known and respected in the community, was trapped! He hid behind the door in embarrassment, indicating to all of us that he needed us to help him out of his predicament.

We became helpless with laughter, all rolling about, just crying with the fun of it all!

Then I came to my senses and realised that, being the mother, I must be polite to these people. So I got up, put on a suitable face and invited them into the dining room for a cup of tea. I asked our guests to sit down and make themselves comfortable while I went to put on the kettle. I then grabbed Bryan's clothes and ran to give them to my poor husband.

Tea was soon forthcoming, and our visitors needed to see the photographs of our work and hear an explanation of what we were doing at ORH. It's not easy to explain such mirth. Not everyone understands that people who have come into a good time of their lives after a bad time can often overreact to any bit of fun that happens.

Another funny incident just before Christmas…

After the lovely new extensions were built, we were able to have a big Christmas tree in the main room. It was very pretty, covered in lights, with baubles and a big star at the top. Some of the people had put little gifts under it, already wrapped, ready for the big day.

Several of us women were chatting in the new kitchen, when one of us said, 'It's gone very quiet. I wonder where the children can be?'

We looked in the big room, and there they were – sitting in a sea of crumpled Christmas paper and string! Lots of little presents littered the floor around them. Pens, cheap perfume, lots of things which had been put there waiting to be opened on Christmas Day.

Little guilty faces looked up at us, in silence. Temptation couldn't be resisted.

We didn't know what to do. To laugh or cry. How would we explain and to whom would we explain? No-one at the house had much money. Those gifts represented considerable sacrifice. We just found a box and put everything in it. We would need to explain to the people when they came in, and hope they would forgive the children, who would have to confess and beg forgiveness when they came. All those little children have children of their own now. Another laugh to add to the others.

To return to the story of Ian... We would have loved to have kept him with us, but it was not to be. Ian had come to us through social services. Sadly, they had already planned his future. We saw his potential after he had been with us just a short while, as he responded to the love and acceptance of everyone at ORH. He enjoyed being useful around the garden and behaved himself very well until he found out that he would have to return to the terrible school where he had been sent as a boarder in term time. Each time Ian went back to school he changed into the troublesome teenager he was reputed to be, and each time he returned to us for the holidays he changed back to be the jolly boy we all knew he was at heart.

The social worker visited Ian regularly. She took him up to his room for private conversations. After one such visit we had trouble. Ian told us that we were forcing him to go to church and become a Christian. Before this, he had come happily to church with us, and there was certainly no pressure of any sort to try to influence his mind. We did pray for him, but he wasn't aware of this. We never tried to make him follow our faith. We left the Holy Spirit to touch his spirit; we knew that only God could do that. We just loved Ian as if we were his parents and friends, which indeed we were.

Ian, however, was stuck between two different attitudes. His school was a very bad influence on him and has been shut down since that time. What must have once been a beautiful old house had deteriorated into a derelict, draughty hole with rats and broken furniture everywhere. I once had to wait outside in the car while one of the other boys took Ian to his room after he had spent the holiday with us. I listened in horror as another poor little boy was being tortured by some big lads in the bushes nearby.

I remember one time we had a phone call from the school to tell us that Ian needed to come home, just the day after he had returned for the new term. He had put his arm through a plate-glass window in a fit of rage. When I went to collect him I saw the window. Once it had been an amazing stained-glass window, on a beautiful staircase in the old house. What a sad fate for what must once have been someone's happy home!

This story is not a happy one. In time Ian reached the school-leaving age. He decided to go to London. Nothing was done by the social services to help him into any sort of employment, so he disappeared into a dark, hidden life as he became independent.

We made contact with Ian's mother and sisters who lived in Portland. They came to see him when he came back to ORH for a visit. Later on, his stepfather and, eventually, his real father came to see him, and he made a reasonable relationship with them all. When Ian had his eighteenth birthday, we arranged a party for him with his family at a local hotel. I have photographs of them all together, playing pool. We all had a very pleasant evening. The following day Ian returned to London.

Ian would arrive 'home' from London at unexpected times. He looked a freak, with terrible punk clothing and wearing chains. It was like something out of a nightmare. We helped him adjust and he soon returned to the happy Ian we knew. But then his 'dark side' would return and he went back to London to a life of drugs and crime. This became a pattern for him, but as time went by he came home less and less often. When we eventually left Old Rectory House in 1990, we thought that he had forgotten us.

One night when we were still at ORH, Bryan and I were woken from a deep sleep, at about midnight, by a London policeman, who told us that we needed to go to London immediately because Ian was threatening to throw himself off a high-rise building. The only person he said he would talk to was Bryan. We quickly dressed and drove to Camden Town as fast as we could. Although we had a London A–Z book, it was a little out of date and we found that some streets had become one-way, and so we became lost. We sat in the car and prayed. There was no-one to be seen, and it was about 3 a.m. Just one person was walking down the street (an angel?) – and we asked him where we were. 'Camden,' he said to us and went on to tell us that we were at the exact location we were looking for.

The outcome was that Bryan persuaded Ian to come down. The policeman, knowing neither Ian nor us, thought he was our son, although we had tried very hard to explain the circumstances. Everyone was very unsympathetic and insisted on arresting Ian, and so they took him away with them. It was such an upsetting event for us all. I think they took Ian to a psychiatric hospital. After a while he came back to ORH and stayed with us for a while, but we could get no evidence as to what had really happened after that time.

Sadly, eventually Ian died from throwing himself off the roof of another high-rise building in London. He was in intensive care for a month before he died. This happened soon after Bryan had died in 1993. Ian had come to Bryan's funeral saying, 'My real father is dead.' He looked very upset, but we all were, of course. I remember that he had a snow-white plait down his back. He looked so freakish on that sad day.

A group of us went to Ian's funeral at Highgate Cemetery. It was a very sad end to a lad with such great potential, but with such a deeply damaged personality from the things he had experienced.

CHAPTER 18

SOME OF THE GIRLS' STORIES

One afternoon a lady brought a beautiful but sad-looking girl to the house. Julie was 17 years old. The lady who brought Julie explained to me that she was a social worker, and Julie had been referred to her by her employer, who was a Christian from the local Baptist church, and with whom Julie had shared a shocking secret. She had grown up thinking all families functioned in the way in which hers did; that her family life was normal. However, a little while previously, Julie had been made to undergo an abortion of twin babies, at twenty-two weeks of gestation. Her stepfather had threatened to strangle her if she didn't tell the doctors that the father of the babies was a boyfriend. What a terrible nightmare she must have gone through. Since the age of 5, Julie's stepfather had regularly been raping her. Apparently, the kindness of her employer, Stella, had prompted Julie to share her secret. She had broken down and cried in her distress.

Stella contacted the college where Julie studied and asked for their social worker's help.

We all sat round the dining room in shock. I heard myself say, 'We need a Christian policeman.' At that very moment the front doorbell rang and there stood the only Christian policeman any of us knew, saying, 'I was just passing by in my car when I felt compelled to pop in and see you.'

It was another miracle – and he was so welcome!

The next visitor was Julie's young sister with a friend, who had walked several miles to come to us when she heard that Julie was with us. In tears she shared the same story. Both sisters were amazed that they were both victims of the same abuse.

Eventually they both told their stories at the police station, and the man concerned went to prison for seven years. (We wished it had been a longer sentence.)

Julie came to live with us for several years. She was very ill for some months, but in due course recovered. We saw how beautiful she really was – all the boys in the house were in love with her and I had a hard job on my hands to keep her safe. She eagerly gave her heart to the Lord, and became a Christian. She was baptised at our local Baptist church, which was a thrill for all of us, especially, no doubt, for Stella, who had first rescued her.

Bryan and I went to Julie's lovely Scottish wedding, and had a wonderful time. She now has a great husband, and is a happy wife and mother of two teenage girls. As a family they foster several other girls because, she says, 'I was fostered once, and being fostered rescued me.'

Another young girl called Genevieve came to us. She had the sweetest little face – so cute! Who could resist it? Certainly not me. She had a pale coffee-coloured skin, framed by dark 'afro' hair. She was a picture made to fall in love with – frail and winsome, so brave and so needy. We were all bowled over by Genevieve.

A social worker arrived with this poor little girl who looked about 8 years old, but was actually nearly 12. She needed a place of safety. Her sad, deranged mother had made her walk all the way from Bournemouth behind an old pram containing everything they owned. She was begging for a bath and some clean clothes when she arrived. We had to dress her in what we could find because she was so small and frail, and she was dressed in only filthy adult clothes wrapped around her skinny body.

Her matted hair was very short, and it was impossible to get a brush or comb through it. She had no idea who her father was, but she said she thought he might have been Jamaican. The social worker (who was one of the few I met whom I really liked, but sadly for us was leaving for the West Country to be married and live there) told us to take Genevieve to the shops the next day and buy clothes and anything she needed. We were asked to keep the receipts and the money would be refunded the following day. What a wonderful outing that was! We saw a new 'Gen' emerge… What a pretty little thing she was.

As Gen's story emerged over the next few weeks, we were horrified that such things could happen, when we thought all our young folk in the UK were safeguarded and well looked after. Gen had been made to walk the streets of Bournemouth every night, trying to escape the 'criminals', as her mother dubbed the policemen. When dawn came, Gen had to crawl into a tiny hole somewhere in Bournemouth station and, bent double, hide all day so that she wouldn't be seen. When they left Bournemouth and eventually arrived in Weymouth after their epic walk, they were apprehended. Gen was sent to the Wey Valley School near where we were living. Her mother then waited in the playground, through every lesson, until the children came out to play or were going home. She would then take Gen away, along with the old pram – we wondered where they had gone.

A good, responsible teacher noticed this was happening and reported it to the authorities, and this was when Gen was brought to us to be in a place of safety.

She soon settled down with us and began to enjoy herself. We all fussed over her, and the other children in the house were very friendly and loving to her. However, I found out one day, when we went to catch the bus to school, that there were bullies at the bus stop, who called out abuse and wanted to harm her. Children can be so cruel. We did all we could to protect her.

Later on, I realised that nothing seemed to affect Gen, either good or bad. She enjoyed a lovely twelfth birthday party in the sunny ORH garden with her new friends. She told us that she had never had a party before. She kept asking me to take her to Bournemouth and when I did she directed me to the Ensbury Park Estate. There we had to watch as she spent at least a couple of frantic hours playing in a children's playground. Later she told me that she used to live in a flat overlooking the park, where her mother piled furniture against the door to stop the 'criminals' from getting in. How sad her story was – the poor little thing had been deprived of everything our children take for granted.

As Gen grew, I began to see that she was really clever. Her school work was exemplary. In her computer work she was top of the class. She could play Bryan's piano as well – even without any lessons. Her sewing and dressmaking was wonderful. She developed a style all her own. It was very 'ethnic' and quite extraordinary. She didn't have much pocket money and so went to charity shops and found clothes which she then remodelled into things she liked, in styles that suited her very well. It was astonishing!

There was something about Gen, though, which began to worry me. She didn't respond to us in a normal manner. She couldn't seem to express love. I talked to her about Jesus and His love for her, and she listened quietly, but that was all. I don't remember ever seeing her cry. I realised that there was damage which only God could deal with. It was certainly beyond my capabilities.

When Bryan and I eventually left ORH we took Gen with us. We gave her a lovely bedroom all to herself. We fussed over her as much as we knew how. We took the dog to the new house, too, so that she could have a friend, and all we asked of her was that she took her out for some walks. I hope she did, although I can't remember her doing so.

The fact was that Gen was angry with us for leaving ORH. She didn't say so, but it was obvious from her behaviour. There was nothing we could do – we were in such distress ourselves, and didn't feel that we could tell her things about the circumstances which would distress her, too. A coolness came over Gen – in fact, an ice-cold attitude developed. By now Bryan was very ill and I had to concentrate on his needs.

Gen's new social worker came to see her and took her to new foster parents in Portland. She hardly said 'goodbye' to us. We didn't see her for a long time, and it nearly broke my heart. No wonder I've got heart problems now that I'm old – it's been broken so many times!

CHAPTER 19

MORE STORIES

What a wonderful man Ethan is! He's an evangelist, telling all who will listen to him about Jesus' love for them.

The first time I saw him, he was in the boys' (young offenders') prison in Portland. The chaplain had asked me to visit him as he had no known relatives, and had made a commitment of his life to Jesus, in his cell. Now, he in turn visits prisons to tell men and boys his story, and how God has changed him.

When I saw Ethan, he was nearing the end of his prison term, and we had been asked to have him at ORH. I asked Matt to come with me on my second visit in order to help me assess him. We agreed that we would ask him to come to us on his first day 'outside'. The offenders were let out for a day, then a weekend, and then a week, to help them adjust to living in the outside world before they were finally discharged.

It was arranged that, for the first day out, I was to meet Ethan in a certain place in town. There were two lads waiting for me when

I arrived, so I took them a long way round, hoping that they wouldn't know where to find us again should they come looking! The other boy was called 'Big Graham'. (He later stayed with us for a while; but I haven't seen him now for a very long time.)

That first day went quite well, so we agreed to have Ethan for the weekend leave, and then he eventually came to stay for a whole year. He was very helpful to Bryan, doing lots of garden jobs. Bryan said he thought he was a really clever boy, although he had not had much formal schooling.

As time went by, he returned to Liverpool and was able to trace his family. He forgave them all and made a new relationship with them. His father came for a holiday with us. The family history was a very sad one, as was usual for so many of our guests.

Ethan met a really nice girl called Catharine, and she became his wife. We held the wedding reception in the ORH garden. In due course they had a lovely daughter, Amanda, who at the time of writing is in Thailand doing charity work.

When Amanda was growing up, Ethan and Catharine fostered other children, so their home was always full.

They had started their married life with nothing, but by now, I guess, they are very wealthy indeed. They started a business, purchasing rundown flats and houses, and improved them dramatically so that people were proud to live in them. The people who live in them are those who had nothing and were unable to raise a deposit. Because Ethan and Catharine had once been in that situation, they trusted their clients. They told me that in all the years only one person had taken advantage of them and let them down. In recent years, Catharine went to university to study law so that she could use her knowledge to help her husband in his work. As I sat talking with them recently, I felt so happy to think that I had been involved in God's plan for Ethan. I hope we will be friends forever!

Another lad, Trevor, had been involved in a car accident. He was only about 20 years old, but he had spent two of those years in hospital as a result of the accident. The first six months of that time he was unconscious. Although he could now live at home, he came to us for holidays so that his parents, who looked after him, could have a rest and a holiday themselves.

Trevor was still very disabled when he first came to us – but we had such fun when he was staying. He was a great character!

The first time he came, he was unable to stand up on his own, but on each subsequent visit he had gained more mobility and he progressed from a wheelchair to a walking aid, and then to a stick. The stick was painted in very lurid, bright colours: purple spots on a yellow background, or in some other amazing and interesting way which he had thought up in order to decorate it.

Trevor could only make sounds at first, not proper speech, and he carried a board with the alphabet on one side and numbers on the other. He would point to each letter as he made up the words which he wanted to say to us. It took a lot of time and was very frustrating if you were in a hurry. Soon, though, he managed to make sounds which were recognisable, so conversation progressed as well. As he had a keen sense of humour and a rather 'rich' vocabulary at times, it was not always advantageous to hear what he was saying!

Poor Trev really needed a girlfriend. He wanted all the girls to kiss him, no matter how old they were. The little children were frightened of him because his face was quite disfigured. This was such a pity and he was very sensitive about it. We tried not to let him know how they felt.

Trevor loved to play cards. He had a pack of huge cards, nearly A5 in size! We often sat and played with him. The games were always very simple ones as he had considerable brain damage and couldn't play complicated ones.

Another thing Trevor loved was to go to the pub, so we endeavoured to take him from time to time. He would order a 'Bloody Mary', which I think is a vodka, and while with us he was limited to one per outing.

One lovely spring evening while he was staying with us, we decided that we would take him out with several of the boys and girls. We took two cars and drove down to Abbotsbury beach. There were a lot of people there, so we changed our plan, and although it had rained quite hard a few days before, we thought we would go a little further along the coast to West Bexington, where there was a very nice pub which we knew would please Trevor. The unmade coast road looked dry enough, but we soon ran into trouble. The mud became deeper and deeper. The second car became stuck and had to be pushed out. As Trevor couldn't get out of the car and I was needed to steer, only he and I were left in it. All the others got behind, and as Bryan shouted 'Push!' they all gave a mighty heave. Alas, the car went forward and everyone else went back, some falling into the mud, and others getting splashed by it. Everyone was wearing their best clothes, which was a shame, but they looked so funny that I cannot help laughing about it even now, all these years later. Of course, it was 'muggins' who had to do all the washing in the next few days!

That night is remembered as a night of disasters. We were really embarrassed to call in at the intended pub with such muddy shoes and clothes; we cleaned them off as best we could and hoped that no-one would notice. No-one did, but Trevor managed to disgrace himself when he pinched a customer's bum, and we were ordered out!

On the way home, for by this time it was dark, one of our cars drove over a badger. We stopped to see if there was anything we could do, but the poor creature was almost, but not quite, dead. A large stone finished the job and put him out of his misery.

What a mad, hilarious, frustrating and distressing evening! I don't think any of us have forgotten it.

One afternoon, Trevor and I were alone in the house, all the other young people being at work or having gone into town. I knew this was very frustrating for him but I had work to do and no time to play the endless card games he always wanted us to play. The doors were open, so it must have been a summer's day. Unknown to me, Trevor quietly got into his wheelchair and disappeared down the drive. I think he intended to try to go to town. I noticed a traffic jam in the road outside the kitchen window, but thought little of it until someone rang the front doorbell.

'Please could you help me with a problem we have in the road?' I was asked. 'There's a young man in a wheelchair stuck right in the middle and no-one can move him. The traffic can't flow until he's out of the way.' The man at the door looked cross and bothered. No wonder! There was Trevor, helpless and paralysed with fear. On either side of him were two large lorries, each with a stream of traffic stuck behind it. I quickly got the chair out of the way and took Trevor back home. I really told him off – tore a strip off him – but he didn't seem to care a bit.

A woman called Jeanette came to stay at one time because she was depressed. Her husband and three children were coping at home while she went to a bedsit in order that she could have 'a bit of space'.

I was not very good with depressed people. I'm afraid I soon ran out of patience, so they often went to my next-door neighbour, Jean, for the sympathy and understanding they needed. Julie was one of these people. She spent a lot of time with Jean. Later Julie decided to go back to her bedsit to sort herself out. Frequent visits to Blackdown House, which was a hospital for people with troubles like hers and was situated just a few doors down the road where she was living, also helped her a lot at this time.

I couldn't seem to help Julie very much, but I did pray for her. I felt that I should write to tell her that she ought to go home to her family. Her husband (who was severely disabled) and children needed her badly. I also told her that she should not indulge in self-pity to the extent that she dragged her family into such suffering. I posted the letter to her bedsit, where I knew she would get it. This was a bold move but one I felt, in this instance, I should take.

That night I woke up sweating in the midst of a terrible nightmare; I can remember it even now. I ran downstairs in the dark and went into the dining room. On the table was a Bible. I opened it at random and read Psalm 116:

> The cords of death entangled me,
>   the anguish of the grave came upon me;
>   I was overcome by trouble and sorrow.
> Then I called on the name of the Lord:
>   'O Lord, save me!'
>
> (verses 3–4)

The psalm spoke to me so powerfully. I was very afraid. Something was going on which I did not understand. There was a spiritual battle in the heavenly realms. I prayed on my knees in agony of spirit.

Julie came back in a day or so. She came to a special service that Sunday, in which we were involved at the church. During the service people were invited to go forward for healing, and Julie went up to the communion rail. She called out loudly in a language we didn't know. It was such a strange time, but Julie became a changed woman. From that time on she had peace in her life. She decided to return home and make her marriage work. A short time later the family all came to ORH for a celebration meal together. I have a photograph which was taken of them all around the table. The children were lovely and Julie's husband was so thankful.

Julie soon became one of our faithful team of helpers. She glows with joy these days. Recently, as I was preparing to go to Romania, I went to the Elim bookshop to buy some things to take with me. There was Julie, smiling and full of grace. She works there now as a volunteer. She bought a lovely carved Christian fish symbol for me to take out to a friend or a church there. She said it was a thanksgiving gift for the happiness she found through what God had done in her life during the time at ORH. It was a real blessing to the man in Romania to whom I gave it, and he took it to his church.

CHAPTER 20

PARTIES AND PUDDINGS

For some strange reason, people began to think that Bryan liked rum and kept giving him bottles. He didn't like the stuff, but had possibly given that impression because he thanked someone who had given him a bottle once at Christmas time. He didn't know what to do with these bottles of rum, so began to put some into the trifles he made for Sunday dinners. They became dubbed 'Captain Morgan's Trifles'. They were certainly enjoyed by everyone. I didn't know what made them so nice, or the atmosphere at Sunday lunch so hilarious at first, but by the time I found out about the rum it was impossible to stop the tradition, so I gave in and enjoyed the trifles, too.

Bryan would make a trifle on Saturday afternoon in a large Pyrex bowl, using any cake that needed finishing up, soaking it in the rum, then adding some tins of fruit, custard and jelly. However large the trifle was, every bit of it was devoured! I have a photograph of 'Big Graham' scraping the bowl.

Christmas Day 1987 was memorable. There were about twenty of us sitting around three tables, which were held together by tablecloths. Bryan sat at the top, carving the enormous turkey. The vegetables and gravy sat at intervals down the tables, along with the mustards and various other condiments. It was a very special 'first' Christmas since the new kitchen and Aga cooker had been installed – and our hopes were very high for the future, after promises of even more improvements to the facilities, as the Cox Trust had some money to spare. Our caring service would surely improve with more help like this. The very latest technology at that time was the lovely new microwave oven which sat proudly in the kitchen, waiting to be used for the first time.

Bryan looked up and said to me, 'I didn't see the Christmas pudding cooking on the Aga, Mags. Where is it?'

'Oh,' I answered, 'I'm going to serve it tomorrow when we'll have a lighter meal, and it'll go down more easily. I made a trifle for today.'

'Oh dear,' he said. 'We *must* have a Christmas pud on Christmas Day!'

So, as everyone was tucking into their lovely dinner, I quietly crept into the kitchen and saw the new microwave oven. It had never been used. So I decided to put the pudding in it to heat it up. Not having had time to read the instructions, I put the pudding into a Pyrex bowl and popped it in, turned the switch to 'high' and set the time for 20 minutes. I went back to finish my meal.

Then someone remarked that they could smell a funny smell coming from the kitchen. I ran out to find a bomb in the microwave, just about to explode! A loud sizzling noise filled my ears and great shoots of steam shot out from all angles. It was frightening! I turned the 'bomb' out on to a plate and ran out with it, shouting, 'Someone open the front door – *quick*!'

I put it on the ground outside, but someone else said, 'Move it away from my car! If it explodes then bits of pudding will spray all over it!'

We all sat round in shock. Sallie Legg, one of us sitting there, had the answer for us all. She took the tea towel she was holding, placed it over her head and moaned, 'I want to bee alooan!'

We all collapsed into laughter at a 'never to be forgotten' event. Just like so many others which happened at ORH.

The house and garden at ORH were a really good venue for wedding receptions. Three of our own family had their receptions in the garden. They usually finished with a disco and loads of fun. The first wedding was a real experience for us all. Our vicar, Revd Richard (Dick) Luther, had a sister, Claire. She and her husband Peter had their wedding reception in the garden in September 1977. It was a very swish, but jolly, affair.

The day before the wedding a large marquee was erected on the lawn in front of the house, with a smaller one for the caterers to attend to all their arrangements.

The bridegroom, Peter, and his best man spent the night before the big day at ORH. Their hired morning suits had already been delivered. Everything seemed to be under control. However, the next morning, we realised that all was not well – chaos threatened. The buttonholes had not arrived, and worse still, Peter could not find his all-important braces or his wedding shoes!

We hunted everywhere for them and many phone calls were made, but to no avail. In the end, the young men walked to the church with Peter wearing garden string around his waist to hold up his trousers, and his old shoes on his feet. Neither of them had a carnation in their lapel. They had to have their photographs taken outside the church without them, as can be seen if one looks at their wedding album. So Peter was married wearing his trousers held up by garden string and in his old shoes!

The flowers arrived after they had left for the church. I ran all the way up to St Ann's Church from ORH carrying a big, flat, wobbly box of carnations (for all the folk who needed them) and the heavy best shoes (by the time I arrived at the church they seemed very heavy, anyway), and also the offending braces!

I was *too late*! We put the flowers in the boys' lapels, but there was no time to fix either the braces or the shoes as the bride's car was arriving at the gate of the church. The shoes and braces were hidden behind a tombstone, and Peter took them back to ORH after the ceremony so that he could change before he greeted his guests.

The team of caterers was headed up by a truly magnificent toast master. He was tall and portly in his morning suit and top hat. (He always reminded me of the Fat Controller in the *Thomas the Tank Engine* books!) When he appeared through the French doors, I innocently asked him, 'Are you one of the caterers?'

He was absolutely *incensed* at this suggestion. He was much too grand for such a humble title.

'I'm the TOAST MASTER,' he replied, in an important voice.

This statement was to become a family joke, which we still use occasionally if we need to explain our 'superiority' in some way.

Well, the toast master duly did his stuff at the appointed time for Claire and Peter. All the guests were seated with their pre-dinner drinks, when our skinny 15-year-old foster son, Paul, thought he would come down to watch the proceedings. He was immediately pounced upon by the intrepid man, who, after asking his name, loudly announced him to all the assembled company.

'MR PAUL STEEPLES!'

Paul has never forgotten this. I think he just wished that a big hole would open up at that moment and swallow him, he was so embarrassed! (He became our son-in-law, the father of our two granddaughters, and a very good and much-loved member of the family.)

When I went up to my room after the bride and groom had left for their honeymoon, there was Claire's beautiful 'Liberty' wedding dress lying on my bed. It was – so her mum, Pat, told me – a very expensive dress. It had cost £100 when it was bought, so would cost at least £1,000 at present-day prices! It was pure white, best-quality cotton, with dainty pintucks all down the bodice. A dress of sheer beauty and grace.

The next morning, we had a lovely visit from our rector, Dick, and his mother Pat, who danced into the kitchen and put a cheque for £100 into my hands. It was quite unnecessary generosity, but was much-appreciated and much-needed finance for us. Pat also tried to make us accept some spare bottles of champagne which had not been opened at the wedding. We declined as we did not need them, but Paul Steeples (no doubt feeling this would be a good way to appease his hurt sensibilities after his brush with the toast master) sneaked a couple of bottles and some glasses up to the boys' attic bedroom.

Later when I went upstairs for something, I heard singing, so went to the attic to see what was happening. I found Paul and Matt, both only 15, absolutely drunk and out of their minds, lying on their beds laughing at me. I saw what they had done and became so angry! I smacked them as if they were naughty little boys. We often laugh about that now.

This was a truly hilarious and joyful wedding. It was a lovely start to all the other wedding receptions we enjoyed at ORH.

CHAPTER 21

MORE SPECIAL EVENTS

Another special wedding which I will never forget was that of Harry and Gwen. Harry came out of hospital to convalesce after a life-threatening chest problem. He seemed as if he were made of tissue paper because he was so delicate. He had not been in the house more than an hour before he was listening to the sad problem of another man, who needed a kind counsellor very much. That was typical of Harry. He was always so aware of other people's needs, and always ready to help them. He really put into practice that saying: 'to be Jesus for people'.

Soon, Gwen came to visit him. Although they were well into their fifties, it was obvious that they were very much in love. Jackie (Matt's wife), coming into the house one day, found them outside in the little front porch, close together. Harry was holding Gwen's face in his hands. It touched Jackie so much to see them like this, in a little world of their own.

Gradually, they shared their story. Harry had endured many years locked into a very unhappy marriage. He used to get up very, very early each day to do the cleaning and make the house spick and span so that his wife had an easy life. Then he went out for the rest of the day so that she didn't have to see him! He was a slave in his own house and all but homeless, too.

Gwen was single. She had sacrificed her whole life to look after her parents. Her mother had died, but we met her father. He seemed to us to be about the most selfish man we had ever met. Still, Gwen cared for his every need, which he didn't seem to notice or appreciate, so long as he had everything he wanted.

The pair shared their problems with their minister and loving friends, who had watched this for many years. They advised Harry and Gwen that they, too, had a right to some life and happiness.

A divorce was arranged for Harry. His wife ended up with everything, not because she was entitled to it, but because he felt he must deny himself everything to give her all she wanted. This left our friends free to get married and enjoy a few happy years together.

What a wedding they had! It was a real celebration. Gwen and Harry were married at Dorford Baptist Church on a lovely April day. No young bride ever looked more lovely than Gwen in her pretty blue suit, and no young man ever looked happier than Harry with his gentle smile.

The wedding reception was held in a marquee on the Old Rectory lawn; all the young folk – Matt, Jackie, Neil, Jacky and several others – dressed themselves as waiters to do the honours at the table. Karen and her team did a wonderful job with the meal, and the joy was palpable as we all sat down to enjoy the feast. Of course, Gwen's old father knew he was the guest of honour, and took all the limelight whenever he could; but Gwen and Harry were so patient with him.

Before the wedding there had been a couple of weeks of rain, but then the sun had come out in all its spring warmth and freshness so that all the daffodils seemed to have blossomed overnight. The lovely chestnut tree also had opened its fresh green leaves, and the flowers, like candles, looked amazing in the sunshine.

After the honeymoon this dear couple lived in Gwen's home, looking after her father until his dying day. Once, a few years after their wedding, Bryan and I were on holiday, picnicking in a remote place in Devon, and we were surprised by a car coming round the corner. It was Harry and Gwen, and they were on holiday, too! Gwen's father had gone into respite care for his own little holiday. We were so glad to see them so very happy together. It wasn't to be for long, because Harry had very poor health and he died soon after that holiday. Gwen also followed him to glory shortly after – she was still relatively young, but would have had no joy in her older years without Harry. I like to think they have ongoing joy in heaven.

Most weeks there was a party or other event at the house or in the garden. If someone had a birthday while they were staying with us, a volunteer would bake a cake and a party was arranged. If the weather made it possible, it would be held in the garden. Adults, even now, remember how much they enjoyed ORH parties! Some of our guests had never been to a party before, let alone had one themselves.

From time to time, we had the day centre arrange to bring their disabled clients and carers for an outing. I remember lots of wheelchairs in the paddock and people enjoying the flowers.

At one time I was given eighty-five Pyrex cups and a huge metal teapot. I always gave cups of tea to groups who came. Most people brought their own picnic food. Many different churches brought groups, and it became a great place for people of different denominations to meet and find that they had much in common. Jesus was making His peace among us all.

Our son, Andy, arranged for some school groups to visit in the evenings. The young people had fun in the river, then came indoors to dry and dress before a barbeque in the paddock around a huge bonfire. (We didn't have all the worries of health and safety rules in those days!) Bryan and I couldn't count the number attending because there were so many. One time, after the parents had collected all the young people, we estimated that we had around 700 visitors that evening!

CHAPTER 22

SOME THOUGHTS AND REFLECTIONS

> I have heard it said that history is written by the winners. Well, I consider myself to be a winner as I write this extraordinary story. However, it ended with personal tragedy; but this could be said of so many people who have answered God's call to service. Think for a moment of what happened to Jesus! We talk glibly about following in His footsteps when we are young; but it leads to a cross. Jesus himself told us to 'take up your cross' – but after the cross came the resurrection. In Him we are always winners!

I know that ORH was just one of many, many projects God has brought into being through the ages; He is still doing just as many miracles now as He ever did for us then.

I often ask Him to do miracles for my brothers and sisters who are in difficult circumstances now: the refugees; those who are being persecuted for their faith; and anyone who is calling out to Him for help. Jesus Christ is alive today, and He's looking after His children as He always has done.

I sat in my chair at the worship service this morning and listened to my son-in-law preach to the congregation at an All Age service. It was powerful stuff. He's a straight-thinking and a straight-talking man. He's from London and there's no nonsense about anything he does – or says. The people responded in delight, but it wasn't the impact of his preaching that was the most thrilling. It was the true faith which shone through. No person sitting there could doubt that Jesus is for him the true God of salvation for mankind, and his own personal Hero and Saviour. Those who knew Paul when as a boy he first came to ORH – an angry, hurt teenager – can only praise the God who has changed his life in such a convincing and amazing way. Earlier in the book I described something of his attitude when we first met him. He was only 15 then; he's over 50 now. I believe that God showed me something at that time of what He would do for him. Paul showed promise even then of being a leader and a role model for many young people, especially for those who were experiencing similar difficulties as they grew up.

I kept a record of the people who came to stay in the house during the twelve years we worked there. The book records that 1,208 people slept in the house over that time. I have only mentioned a few of them, as their stories would fill far too many books! I wish I had also kept a record of the number of parties, picnics, evening get-togethers and wedding receptions which were held and enjoyed in the garden in the summer and the house in the winter, but sadly I didn't. I was so busy, there just wasn't time to do that. Altogether, there were approximately two parties or picnics a week. So many came; at times we were inundated with people – the tired, the hurting and the needy. Some walked miles to us because they heard there were people in ORH who could help them. One lady arrived, exhausted, on our doorstep. She had walked all the way from South Wales. She wanted to make her family listen and look at the problem they faced within their family structure. After a few phone calls and lots of prayer, she was on her way home again. Later she wrote to tell us they had all made amends and she wanted us to know that things had improved.

But sadly, there were others who were not genuine, but came to use us. There were intractable liars; alcoholics; drug abusers, using glue and LSD, and injecting heroin; thieves; the unforgiving, angry people who were inwardly thirsting for revenge. Sadly, some were downright obnoxious people. We needed to pray constantly as they told us their stories. Many had mental health issues and instability resulting from their lifestyles. Our psychiatric hospitals treat many such people, and kind medical staff try to help, but we know that only Jesus has the true and lasting answer.

Prayer was our strength and help in every situation. It was the mainstay of ORH. If we didn't pray, then we knew things wouldn't go well. When we did, the answer wasn't always what we expected, but later, something better would happen, and that was amazing!

CHAPTER 23

CONCLUSION

I wonder sometimes how many other people, who followed God's call and put their lives on the line, risking all to do what they sincerely believed He was calling them to do, felt in the end that they had come to a point of disaster, after all their efforts? That was how we felt. It is an oft-repeated story through the years, is it not? It has always been and always will be a spiritual battle, and it seems to us at times that we have lost; but take heart – in fact we have won!

We followed Jesus – and for Him, it seemed once as if He had lost, but in the end He won, He was victor! After the cross comes the crown. It has always been worthwhile to follow Him, no matter what the cost.

In Jesus, we will never fail. 'Failure' is a word we will never acknowledge. Dangers, yes; but the dangers we face are glorious when we follow the call of love.

On 20 September 1988, Bryan and I sat at a picnic table on the lawn of ORH waiting for the answer we had to demand from our parochial church council (PCC). We had waited all summer to receive it. We were still taking people in, even though we were both exhausted and needing more help.

We had expected to be involved with the people in the church when it came to making decisions about the future of the work at ORH. We knew how valuable it was. We had been told on good authority that the Cox Trust, which was a large legacy recently left to our church, would continue to fund the work.

Our great need was for another couple or a small group of people to come alongside and work with us, with the expectation that they, in due course, would take over the ministry and allow us to step down, leaving them free to continue it in their own way and fulfil their own vision for the needs of the people who continued to come, even though we sometimes had tried to say we were 'shut'. It was impossible to shut the house when so many needy people continued to arrive asking for help. Such help was really desperately needed in our very stressful society – and indeed, the need is still there even as I write this twenty-five years later.

We were prepared for the PCC to come up with new ideas and suggestions for the work in which we had been involved for the past twelve years. We acknowledged that we had made many mistakes. Who in this life doesn't, however hard they try to listen to what the Lord says to them and obey sincerely?

When a hard, formal report came from the PCC, it shocked us so much that we were paralysed with the deepest dismay. The work of ORH was not even mentioned. There was no mention of the people who had been coming to get comfort and understanding for so long now.

The report only spoke of the building and its use. It was absolutely dismissive of our ideas and vision. There was no mention of praying for the Holy Spirit to guide us in what decisions we might make. It was just a business decision, with no account of what the Lord wanted. I knew that the people making these decisions had never come to visit the house when it was buzzing with life, or come to ask if they could help.

Perhaps, I began to think, could this be motivated by jealousy? Were we so successful at ORH that others could not bear to see the house like a beehive of happy activity, with healing happening in so many lives?

The report had no mention of the people who came for help because they couldn't trust the institution of the church; no mention of the nights when we had to get up and rescue someone who had phoned us in distress, even though the next morning Bryan had to get up and go to work in order to bring in the money needed to support us and others, who had no way of paying for their keep. There was also no mention of the part ORH had taken with other churches in the area to promote true Christian unity.

The report just stated that the house should be put to another use, other than that in which we had been engaged for the past twelve years. It suggested that it would make a good conference centre! Would it? It would never have been accepted for that use by the powers who ran the local authority. No research had been undertaken as to the viability of that suggestion. Bryan was a planning officer for the town council and he knew that such an idea was just not possible. There was no access for a large number of vehicles or for a large number of people to reside there. We had used it as an extended family home. The only way that a house like that could be used for any group was as an extended family home. That is one reason why we had never tried to change it.

After listening to many empty explanations given to try and justify the report, we grew very tired and confused, feeling betrayed by our dear friends in the church, whom we had trusted for so many years, and we became despondent.

I began to be angry. I saw my lovely, hard-working Bryan begin to look ill. In fact, he was like an old man. Something I had never realised that I was capable of started to build up inside me. It was anger – real anger!

I walked around the place looking at all the things we had worked so hard to provide, to make the home such a welcoming and warm place for everyone who came. After all, I reasoned, it wasn't the house which was important, but it was the work which went on inside it.

We had been completely misunderstood. We had heard people say that we, the Dukes' family, were enjoying the lifestyle of the rich down there in that lovely setting. (In today's language: *I wish!*) These were certainly people who had never been to visit when the sad and difficult guests had brought their traumas in.

After the review was given to us, we were so upset and it made us feel as if God had forgotten us. What had we done wrong? As Bryan slept I found myself waking up in the early hours of the morning and creeping downstairs in the dark. I sat in the lovely old rocking chair that was always kept beside the Aga cooker. I felt so confused, and prayed to God in my distress.

'How could they do it?' I asked Him. I felt as if I was the most badly treated person that ever had to face such things. Gently, the answers came. Very quietly, He began to talk to me. I listened, spellbound, trying to understand. It was just like when I sat on the steps in the front of the house before we started the work.

'I was misunderstood,' He said. 'This is the way of the cross.' I can't remember all He said to me on those nights, but I knew then that I was safe in His hands, and it was all in His control.

Then I began to think about what happened to Jesus – how they arrested Him on a trumped-up charge. They made Him stand before the 'powers that be' in their government. Pilate washed his hands because he was frightened of Him, and secretly knew His authority. The soldiers tied Him to a pillar and flogged Him. Some spat in His face and hit Him. They pushed a crown of thorns on His head and laughed to see the blood pouring down. Then they murdered Him – in the most brutal way they knew how. They made the Roman soldiers of the invading army do their dirty work. Then they laid Him on a rough piece of wood fashioned into a cross and hammered big, rusty nails through His hands and feet. They put the cross up between two criminals. Then they stood around and jeered and called out horrible suggestions, like, 'If you are the Son of God, come on down from there. You did it for others, but you cannot do it for yourself!'

I wondered who the 'they' were. Are we not just as guilty? Every time we sin, we hurt our Heavenly Father. We have no reason to point the finger. We are all sinners, too.

Even in such agonising pain, Jesus didn't forget His mother. He made provision for her to be looked after by His friend. Now that I'm an old mother, how much I appreciate His gesture! He looks after me, too.

After Jesus died, His friends laid Him in a cave – but He didn't stay dead!

He rose again. He is the firstborn from the dead.

He's alive now – still, and He always will be. His Spirit is living in every person who believes in Him.

He's living in me. Is He living in you? Just ask Him and He will come to you!